THE GREAT BRITISH
BAKE OFF®

Kitchen
Classics

THE GREAT BRITISH
BAKE OFF®

Kitchen
Classics

Signature bakes from
the heart of the home

SPHERE

Contents

A note from Paul

I come from a long line of bakers. Not only does that mean that 'baking' and 'home' are words that, to me, belong together like 'bread' and 'flour' or 'pastry' and 'filling', it means that I've spent my entire life watching baking transform and innovate in front of my eyes. I find it endlessly fascinating, inspiring and exciting to see how traditional bakes can be reinvented – and it's a privilege that I get, as part of my day job, to be even a short piece of the evolving baking story; one that has been so fundamental to my family for decades.

The combination of old and new, familiar and fresh, classic and contemporary is at the core of *The Great British Bake Off* in 2023. Each year we discover incredible stories behind the bakers' passions, but this year has blown me away. With a brief to add a fresh twist to the classic recipes we all know and love, the bakers created truly awe-inspiring signature dishes. Their creations don't just update old favourites, but – like all the best bakes – reveal stories about the people behind them. From beloved family recipes that add a twist with each new generation, to older classics being revived and brought up to date, we have loved getting to know the 2023 bakers through what they make in the kitchen.

This is the inspiration for our 2023 *Bake Off* book. In its pages, you'll find recipes for Signature Bakes that will sit proudly on the kitchen table, with crowd-pleasing appeal. What could be better than a collection of bakes that epitomise the joy of the kitchen? With biscuits and breads; pastries and patisseries, desserts, chocolate inventions, and, of course, cakes, these are recipes we know you'll want to make at home. I'm also sure that combining the comfort of classics with inventive and exciting twists makes this a book you'll come back to again and again.

A note from Prue

I have judged *The Great British Bake Off* for seven years now, and you'd think I'd have had enough of eating cake! But the skill of the bakers, and the effort, imagination and passion they put into their baking, endlessly fascinates me. Year after year, our bakers are delightful and interesting, and they somehow quickly become a gang of friends. They never try to undermine each other, they will jump to and help other bakers in trouble, and they are brave and uncomplaining when it's time for them to go home. There must surely be magic in the tent!

The other reason I love *Bake Off* is because the recipes are so good and the bakes delicious. Who wouldn't want a job eating amazing breads, wonderful pies and fantastic cakes?

I love it that, as a breed, chefs and cookery writers are continually experimenting with flavours, new ingredients, other peoples' cuisines. But sometimes an old favourite, or an absolutely classic recipe, just fits the bill. For the 2023 series, we concentrated on the classics, but, in true *Bake Off* tradition, we asked the bakers to adapt those classics as they wished, to give them an original twist. I had my doubts that some old favourites *could* be improved upon, but of course, the bakers rose to the challenge magnificently. The 2023 bakers came up with ideas that were fresh, new and exciting, while remaining faithful to the comfort of each familiar, much-loved classic.

Of the three *Bake Off* challenges, I find the Signature Bake the most satisfying. The recipes are not as elaborate and time-consuming as the Showstopper, and they are based on the kind of bakes we all love to make at home – which makes them eminently achievable. And this is what this book is about: Signature Bakes each with a *Bake Off* twist. All you need to do is to follow the recipes faithfully and, I promise you, they will not disappoint. You will have achieved a classic bake, worthy of a place in the *Bake Off* tent.

Introduction

Welcome to *The Great British Bake Off: Kitchen Classics,* a collection of sweet and savoury bakes from Paul, Prue and the team behind the show, as well as, of course, the 2023 bakers themselves.

Every year, as we begin thinking about the series and the book to accompany it, there is excited discussion about what themes or passions might reveal themselves in the bakers' ideas and recipes. In 2023, overwhelmingly, we saw a real buzz about taking a traditional bake, looking at it with fresh eyes and giving it a modern twist. In that vein, then, this book is all about 'signature' bakes that you will probably already know and love, but each one is reimagined with uplift. Put simply, it is a collection of 72 recipes that make the ordinary extraordinary.

A CLASSIC EVOLUTION

It's well known that baking has been around for thousands of years. But that doesn't mean that it has stood still. Taking an original and adapting it according to improved understanding and techniques, changing palates and better availability of ingredients defines the evolution of all cooking. If you asked the ancient Egyptians for their signature loaf (way back in about 2,600BCE), you'd be offered a simple mixture of dried and pounded grain and water (a sludgy gruel), left to 'bake' on a hot stone to create a sort of primitive flat bread. Several millennia later, after the discovery of yeast, the ancient Romans had evolved *panis quadratus,* a kind of barely risen sourdough, baked into eight segments to create a Caesar-style tear-and-share. Later still, Medieval Europeans were baking fruit breads and gingerbreads that are now considered early forms of 'cake'. The sponge as we know it today, though,

became recognisable only after 1843, when a Gloucestershire chemist named Alfred Bird combined bicarbonate of soda with cream of tartar and cornflour to create baking powder. With this huge leap in baking science – and as trade routes with Africa, South America and the Middle East opened up our palates to flavourings such as vanilla, chocolate and citrus – a basic sponge turned into an edible canvas, an opportunity for every baker to add their own artistry in the form of flavour, decoration and style, just as it continues to be today. (As if to prove the proverbial pudding, pastry enjoyed a similar evolution: from a simple mixture of flour, oil and water in ancient Egypt, through Medieval pie crusts to the delicate, laminated, crispy and crumbly doughs of 19th-century French patisserie – and beyond.)

At no time in history, then, has baking stood still, and if *Bake Off* teaches us anything, it's that there continues to be so much to learn. Invention and reinvention define our show: when our bakers look back to the classics that might have inspired them to pick up a balloon whisk in the first place, we sense an instinct to see what else their imaginations and skills are capable of. It's alchemy for modern times.

USING THIS BOOK

The idea that the recipes should represent signature bakes with interesting twists and innovations immediately lent itself to organising the chapters in this book according to some of our most popular signature weeks: Cake, Biscuits, Bread, Pastry, Patisserie, Dessert, Chocolate and Free-from have all tested the knowledge and skills of our bakers in fundamental ways. The weeks have also demonstrated just how creative and interesting classics can be when flair and imagination come into play. It's in these chapters that you'll find a pistachio cake with vertical layers (page 27), a tie-dye party ring (page 56), a flavour-flecked burger bun (page 91), a hazelnut frangipane pear tart (page 122), an exquisitely fruity berry Charlotte (page 147), an elegant, sliced trifle (page 159), a chocolate 'brookie' (page 189) and delicate, finely piped macarons (page 214), to highlight a few.

Every recipe has been taken from its origins and given a modern makeover, and we hope that as you make your way through the bakes, you'll be encouraged to see what masterpieces you can create in your own kitchen. To help stir up your own creativity, at the end of the book is a special section that collects together some of the Original Kitchen Classics that provide the blank canvas for at least one (often more) of the 72 chapter recipes. In this end section are the recipes for eight essential bakes that in some way define each signature style. So, while the Cake chapter heralds a four-tier, Lemon, Lime & Blackberry Victoria Sponge (page 20), the original kitchen classic offers up its humble beginnings – a simple Victoria sponge with jam and buttercream filling (page 218). Similarly, the Pecorino, Walnut & Rosemary Shortbreads on page 67 are a reimagining of the classic, even biscuit-defining Scottish shortbread recipe on page 219. And so on.

The book finishes with 'Inspire me', which reorganises all of our 72 bakes into the time of day and circumstances for which you might choose to whip them up. Of course, there are no hard-and-fast rules here: if you want to tuck into a Gooey Chocolate Caramel Tart (page 185) for breakfast, we won't argue. No, the whisk is yours when it comes to choosing which recipe to bake and for what reason, but if you need inspiration, pages 241–51 are there to offer a gentle, guiding hand.

NOTES ON THE RECIPES

Oven temperatures: Ovens vary – not only from brand to brand, but from the front to the back of the oven, as well as (in a non-fan oven) between the top and bottom shelves. Invest in an oven thermometer if you can, which will give you a more accurate reading of the heat in your oven. Always preheat the oven, and use dry oven gloves.

Eggs: Eggs are medium and should be at room temperature, unless specified. Some recipes may contain raw or partially cooked eggs. Pregnant women, the elderly, babies and toddlers, and people who are unwell should be aware of these recipes.

Butter: In the recipes, 'softened butter' means to soften to room temperature, unless otherwise specified. 'Softened' means you should be able to leave an indentation with your fingertip when you press down.

Herbs, vegetables and fruit: Use fresh herbs and fresh, ripe, medium-sized vegetables and fruit unless the recipe specifies otherwise.

Spoon measures: All teaspoons and tablespoons are level unless otherwise stated.

Waxed citrus: When a recipe calls for citrus zest, it's preferable to use unwaxed fruit. However, some citrus, such as grapefruits and blood oranges, are hard to find unwaxed. In this case, before zesting, place the fruit in a colander, pour over boiling water, then dry the fruit thoroughly to remove the waxy residue.

Allergies or special diets: We want you to share these recipes with your loved ones and your community as often as possible. Please be aware, though, that some recipes contain allergens. If you are baking for others, do check before you share – there is a delicious collection of allergy-friendly recipes in the Free-from chapter on pages 196–215.

ABBI
Cumbria
Veg grower &
delivery driver
• • • • • •

Yorkshire-born Abbi first
learned to bake alongside
her mum, honing those early
skills during her teens, when
she became enthralled by the
Victorian era and especially
the traditional bakes of the
time – steamed puddings,
fruit cakes and more. Now
she takes her inspiration
from her environment
and the beautiful English
countryside around her home.
A lover of the great outdoors,
she forages for seasonal
ingredients – the bigger and
bolder, the better – and puts
her homegrown veg to good
use. Abbi's bakes aim to
combine comfort and
familiarity with a strong
nod towards nature, and a
feeling of creating something
magical – bakes with a touch
of fairytale!

AMOS
North London
Deli & grocery
manager
• • • • • •

Film and theatre enthusiast,
theme-park lover and
hospitality professional,
Amos grew up in Nottingham
with his mum and sister, but
now lives and works in North
London. As a child, Amos was
always amazed by his mum's
ability to whip up delicious
bakes at a moment's notice
– making her both the
inspiration and the role model
for his own commitment to
some serious baking. Amos
describes his bakes as a
labour of love – his style
is colourful and chic with
keen attention to detail, and
he loves exploring different
flavour profiles. He compares
his baking style to the
converted church that he
now lives in, calling both his
style and home 'traditional
with a modern twist'.

CRISTY
East London
Mum & PA
• • • • • •

Life with four children means
that, for Cristy, there always
seems to be a birthday to
bake for and an exciting party
to plan. She describes her
baking style as enchanted
and pretty – bakes that
conjure up a sense of
childhood. Cakes are her
speciality, and she draws
flavour inspiration from
her own Israeli heritage and
from her husband's Jamaican
roots. She is a dab hand with
decoration and gets a thrill
out of making sure the results
look perfect. When she's not
organising a celebration,
you can find her having an
outdoor adventure, letting
her hair down with her
friends, or solving a Rubik's
cube – in under 4 minutes!

DAN
Cheshire
Civil engineering
resource planner
• • • • •

Dan's interest in cooking began when he went travelling in South America in 2007. His particular loves are pies and puddings: before he and his wife bought their first home, they lived with his in-laws, during which time his mother-in-law taught him how to make perfect shortcrust pastry. Subsequently, his passion for pies has evolved into a penchant for patisserie! Perfectionist Dan loves a baking challenge and will often find the hardest bake in one of his many (more than 300!) cook books and start there, throwing everything he's got at creating a masterpiece. When he's not baking, he loves to play football with his two young sons, work out in the gym, or forage for edible treats in the countryside around his home.

DANA
Essex
Database
administrator
• • • • •

Dana's passion for baking started at the age of 16 when she identified a gap in her family's traditionally Indian culinary repertoire. As a self-professed untidy baker, Dana would avoid stepping on her mum's toes in the kitchen by catching the bus to her dad's house to indulge her need to experiment with her bakes. Now she has a kitchen of her own (and a cockapoo, Gracie, to clean up after her), Dana has become the family's go-to celebration cake-maker. Her style is rustic and homely, but always pleasing to the eye. She loves a semi-naked cake with neat lines, pretty piping and minimalist decoration; and although she likes to keep her flavours safe, Dana will often incorporate a twist or two, adding in familiar spices associated with her Indian heritage.

JOSH
Leicestershire
Post-doctoral
research associate
• • • • •

Josh is a chemist by trade and brings his scientist's precision and keenness to experiment into the kitchen, taking careful notes on each part of the baking process and perfecting all his techniques for gorgeous results. He likes to take his inspiration from old baking books, reinventing classics to give them a modern twist, often by introducing alternative flavours and including the seasonal fruit and vegetables from his kitchen garden. Josh has been playing rugby for his local team for more than 15 years, and once a month he bakes lots of treats to reward his teammates after a rigorous training session. He dreams of having his own artisan bakery one day.

KEITH
**Hampshire
Chartered
accountant**

• • • • • •

Apple pies and fairy cakes – which he learned to bake with his mum – form the baking backdrop to Keith's childhood, along with his mum's love for traditional dishes from her home in Malta. Since those formative years, Keith has never stopped baking. Recently, though, he has returned to the baking books of the early 1970s to attempt recipes that were once 'beyond' him. He loves the challenge of taking on more complex bakes and has grown in confidence with bread. His partner, Sue, has got very used to waking up to the smell of a freshly baked loaf! They live with their poodle, Maisie, just a few steps from the sea.

MATTY
**Cambridgeshire
PE & science
teacher**

• • • • • •

Matty is the type of baker who swats up on online patisserie videos before bed. No matter how good he gets, though, he strives to equal the impressiveness of the bake that first caught his imagination: a teddy-bear cake that his late nan made him for his fourth birthday. Now the family's designated baker, he always has a list of cake requests for upcoming celebrations. He describes his style as rustic but neat, and his flavour preferences as quite traditional – he particuarly loves chocolate, citrus and nuts. Once his days in the tent are over, his next – and even bigger – challenge will be to make his own wedding cake, a special commission from his fiancée, Lara.

NICKY
**West Midlands
Retired cabin crew
& volunteer**

• • • • • •

Nicky describes her baking as 'like a pair of comfy old slippers; little traditional bakes that evoke fond memories'. For Nicky herself, those memories are of her Gran's kitchen table where, as a little girl, she would roll out pastries and decorate cakes – which she says was as much fun then as all her baking is to her now. Her favourite bakes are still pastries, but she also loves making breads, and fun birthday cakes for her niece and grandchildren. When she's not baking, Nicky volunteers for a pet-therapy charity (along with her dog, Bracken) and loves to ski, which she has been doing since she was only three years old.

ROWAN
West Yorkshire
Student
· · · · · ·

'Go big, or go home' is Rowan's motto, and one that he has always applied to his bakes. His earliest baking memories are of scones, pork pies, shortbread and traditional jam tarts (which he claims as a Northern delicacy). A student of English literature, when he's not writing up a storm, Rowan is also a keen host, applying his creative eye to his cooking – he aims for clean lines and interesting decoration in his finished bakes. Just like his much-admired, knock-out cocktail-making skills, Rowan expresses his grand, opulent side in his bakes, wowing his uni friends with his creations. He made his own 21st birthday cake – a three-tier, 12-layer extravaganza.

SAKU
Herefordshire
Intelligence analyst
· · · · · ·

Sri Lankan-born Saku places the traditional flavours of her heritage at the heart of her baking – particularly the curry spices, which she claims make for the best pie fillings, while liberal sprinklings of cinnamon, cardamom and nutmeg find their way into her sweeter bakes. At her family home in Sri Lanka, Saku didn't have an oven until she was 18, so she turned to baking only when she moved with her husband to the UK, in 2003, and particularly when she became a mum – rustling up treats for her children's lunchboxes by replicating the snacks she saw in the supermarket. Self-taught, she is now a dab hand with a whisk and relishes using her homegrown ingredients from her pride and joy – her vegetable patch.

TASHA
Bristol
Participation officer
· · · · · ·

The best thing Tasha remembers about baking as a child was licking the sugar icing from the tops of the fairy cakes she, her mum and her grandma used to make. At secondary school, she made cakes for her friends and was soon encouraged by her Food Technology teacher to develop her skills as a hobby. Much like her attitude to life, Tasha's baking is fearless. She uses it as a way to express herself creatively, often embarking upon near-impossible designs – with impressive results! When she's not baking, Tasha loves going to the theatre to see a West End show and she has a passion for travelling the world.

1
Cake

Lemon, lime & blackberry Victoria sponge

Serves: 10
Hands on: 2 hours + cooling
Bake: 30 mins

FOR THE LEMON AND LIME CURD
juice and finely grated zest
    of 1 unwaxed lemon
juice and finely grated zest
    of 1 unwaxed lime
1 egg
2 egg yolks
100g caster sugar
65g unsalted butter, cubed
pinch of salt

FOR THE SPONGES
125g unsalted butter,
    cubed and softened
250g caster sugar
1 tsp vanilla paste
125g double cream,
    at room temperature
3 eggs, lightly beaten
1 egg yolk
300g self-raising flour
½ tsp baking powder
pinch of salt
3 tbsp whole milk

FOR THE FILLING
200g blackberries, fresh,
    or frozen and defrosted
50g caster sugar, plus 2 tbsp
juice of ½ lime
475ml double cream
1 tbsp icing sugar, sifted,
    plus extra for dusting
150g blackberries and strawberries,
    sliced, to decorate

You will need
18cm round cake tins x 2, greased,
    then base-lined with baking paper
medium piping bag fitted with
    a large star nozzle

Made with half butter and half double cream, this Victoria sponge has an extra-delicate, but rich crumb. It has four tiers, layered with lashings of cream, tangy curd and fruity blackberry compôte. A simple cake made fit for a queen!

. . . .

1 **Make the lemon and lime curd.** Whisk both citrus juices and zests, egg, yolks and sugar in a heatproof bowl to combine. Place the bowl over a pan of gently simmering water. Add the butter and salt and cook, stirring, for 10 minutes, until the mixture thickly coats the back of a spatula. Pass the curd through a sieve into a clean bowl, cover the surface with a disc of baking paper and leave to cool. Chill until ready to use.

2 **Make the sponges.** Heat the oven to 180°C/160°C fan/Gas 4. Beat the butter, sugar and vanilla in a stand mixer fitted with the beater, on medium speed for 2 minutes, scraping down the inside of the bowl from time to time, until the mixture is pale and creamy. Add the cream in a steady stream, mixing on low for 1 minute, until light and creamy. A little at a time, add the eggs and yolk, beating well between each addition. Sift in the flour, baking powder and salt. Add the milk and mix again to combine.

3 Divide the mixture equally between the prepared tins and spread it level. Bake the sponges for 25–30 minutes, until risen, golden and a skewer inserted into the centre of the sponges comes out clean. Leave to cool in the tins for 5 minutes, then turn them out onto a wire rack to cool completely.

4 **Make the filling.** Meanwhile, tip the blackberries into a small pan, add the 2 tablespoons of caster sugar and cook on a low–medium heat for 10 minutes, stirring occasionally, until it is the consistency of a soft-set jam. Transfer to a bowl and leave to cool.

5 Tip the 50g of sugar into a pan. Add the lime and 2 tablespoons of water and bring to the boil. Reduce the heat and simmer for 1 minute to a light syrup. Leave to cool. Whip the cream with the icing sugar to firm peaks and spoon half into the piping bag.

6 **Assemble the cake.** Cut each sponge horizontally in half, giving four layers. Set aside one of the top layers. Brush the top of the remaining three layers with the lime syrup. Place one layer on a serving plate and pipe a ring of cream around the top edge. Fill the middle of the ring with half of the curd and spread it level. Top with the second sponge layer. Pipe a ring of cream and this time fill the middle with the blackberry compôte. Cover with the third layer, and repeat the cream and curd. Top with the final sponge, cut-side down, and spread over the remaining cream. Arrange the berries on top and dust with icing sugar.

Prue's lemon & thyme bundt

Serves: 12
Hands on: 1 hour
Bake: 40 mins

FOR THE SPONGE
325g unsalted butter, cubed
    and softened, plus extra
    melted for greasing
325g caster sugar
5 eggs
325g self-raising flour
1 tsp baking powder
finely grated zest of
    3 unwaxed lemons
4 tbsp thyme leaves
juice of 1 lemon

FOR THE LEMON-THYME SYRUP
juice of 2 lemons
100g caster sugar
small bunch of thyme

**FOR THE CRYSTALLISED
LEMON AND THYME**
1 unwaxed lemon
100g caster sugar, plus
    extra for sprinkling
1 egg white, beaten
5 thyme sprigs

FOR THE ICING
150g icing sugar
juice of ½ lemon

You will need
23cm 10-cup bundt tin
1 baking sheet, lined with
    baking paper

This is no ordinary lemon sponge. Combining lemon juice with thyme gives the bundt a heady, botanical quality. Don't hold back on the thyme – the recipe calls for a lot, and (because of it) the results are out of this world.

1 **Make the sponge.** Heat the oven to 180°C/160°C fan/Gas 4. Generously grease the bundt tin with melted butter, making sure you brush it between the grooves to prevent the sponge sticking when you turn it out.

2 Beat the butter and sugar in a stand mixer fitted with a beater, on medium speed for 3–5 minutes, scraping down the inside of the bowl from time to time, until the mixture is pale and creamy. One at time, add the eggs, beating well between each addition, and adding a spoonful of the flour if the mixture starts to curdle.

3 Sift the flour and baking powder into the bowl and mix on a low speed until combined.

4 Add the lemon zest and thyme leaves and mix until combined. Stir in the lemon juice to give a thick dropping consistency.

5 Spoon the mixture into the prepared bundt tin and, using a spatula, gently push the batter into the grooves and up the sides of the tin, then smooth the top. Tap the tin on the work surface to release as many air bubbles as possible. Bake the sponge for 35–40 minutes, until risen and golden, and a skewer inserted into the centre comes out clean.

6 **Make the lemon-thyme syrup.** While the sponge is baking, pour the lemon juice into a small pan, add the sugar and bring to the boil. Add the thyme, turn the heat down slightly and simmer for 10 minutes, until the liquid has reduced to a syrup consistency. Pass the syrup through a sieve into a bowl and leave it to cool. Discard the thyme.

7 **Make the crystallised lemon.** Using a potato peeler, peel the lemon in strips, running from top to bottom, then cut the lemon peel into matchsticks. Place the peel in a small pan, cover with water and bring the water to the boil. Immediately remove the pan from the heat and pass the water through a sieve. Tip the lemon matchsticks back into the pan and repeat the boiling and draining process once more to get rid of any bitterness in the peel.

8 Place the drained lemon matchsticks in a pan with the 100g of caster sugar and 100ml of water and bring to the boil. Turn the heat down slightly and simmer for 15 minutes, until the peel

Continues overleaf

Prue's lemon & thyme bundt
continued

strips are translucent and soft. Pass them through a sieve, then spread the strips out on the lined baking sheet and sprinkle them with sugar. Toss to coat each piece of lemon peel in the sugar.

9 **Make the crystallised thyme.** Pour the egg white into a shallow dish and lay the thyme sprigs in it. One by one, remove the sprigs and wipe them almost dry with kitchen paper. Place them next to the lemon peel and sprinkle with sugar. Leave the sheet in a warm place for the thyme and lemon peel to dry and crystallise for at least 2–3 hours.

10 Meanwhile, remove the bundt from the oven and leave it to cool in the tin for 5 minutes, then turn it out onto a wire rack.

11 While the sponge is still warm, use a thin skewer to prick holes over the surface and brush with the lemon-thyme syrup. Be patient and allow the syrup to sink into the sponge before adding more, then leave the bundt to cool completely.

12 **Make the icing.** Sift the icing sugar into a bowl and add enough lemon juice to mix to a stiff, but pourable icing (you may not need all the juice). Spoon the icing over the bundt cake, leaving it to drip down the ridges, and then decorate with the crystallised lemon and thyme.

Pistachio & raspberry vertical cake

This showstopper of a cake seems to defy everything we know about layered sponges with its vertical pink-and-green stripes. A touch of green food colouring enhances the effect – but do go easy. The tangy buttercream, flavoured entirely with fresh raspberry purée is so light as to be mousse-like.

Serves: 10
Hands on: 2 hours + chilling
Bake: 30 mins

FOR THE SPONGES
80g unsalted butter, melted,
    plus extra for brushing
130g plain flour, plus extra
    for dusting
8 eggs
200g caster sugar, plus 2 tbsp
    for sprinkling
2 tsp finely grated unwaxed
    lemon zest
2 tsp vanilla paste
green food-colouring paste (optional)
1 tsp baking powder
100g ground pistachios
2 pinches of salt

FOR THE RASPBERRY PURÉE
400g raspberries
50g caster sugar
juice of ½ lemon

FOR THE BUTTERCREAM
325g caster sugar
5 egg whites
pinch of salt
375g unsalted butter,
    cubed and softened
1 tsp vanilla paste

TO DECORATE
fresh raspberries
nibbed unsalted pistachios

You will need
33 x 23cm Swiss roll tin, greased,
    then lined (base and sides)
    with baking paper
2 baking sheets
piping bag fitted with a medium
    star nozzle

1 Heat the oven to 180°C/160°C fan/Gas 4. Brush the baking paper of the prepared Swiss roll tin with melted butter, then dust with flour and tip out any excess.

2 **Make the sponges.** You will need to make the sponges in two batches, using half of the ingredients at a time. Whisk 4 eggs and 100g of sugar in a stand mixer fitted with the whisk, on medium speed for 2–3 minutes, until trebled in volume, and the mixture leaves a firm ribbon trail when you lift the whisk. Whisk in 1 teaspoon of lemon zest and 1 teaspoon of vanilla and a tiny dot of green food-colouring paste, if using, until combined.

3 Sift in 65g of the flour and ½ teaspoon of baking powder, then, using a large metal spoon, fold in 50g of the ground pistachios and a pinch of salt. Pour 40g of the melted butter around the inside edge of the bowl and fold it into the mixture. Pour the mixture into the prepared Swiss roll tin and gently spread it level, trying not to knock out too much air or volume.

4 Bake the sponge on the middle shelf for 15 minutes, until risen and golden, and the top is firm and springy when gently pressed with a fingertip. Leave the sponge to cool for 3 minutes, then sprinkle 1 tablespoon of caster sugar evenly over the top.

5 Lay a clean sheet of baking paper on top of the sponge and a large baking sheet on top of that. Carefully flip the sponge over onto the baking sheet and peel off the lining paper. Using the clean sheet of baking paper to help, roll the sponge into a spiral, starting at one of the short sides and with the paper inside the roll. This helps to 'train' the sponge for rolling later. Leave to cool, while you reline the baking sheet and repeat steps 2 to 5 for the second sponge, then leaving that to cool, too.

6 **Make the raspberry purée.** Cook the raspberries with the sugar and lemon juice in a pan on a low heat for 10 minutes, stirring often, until you have a juicy slump. Press the mixture through a nylon sieve into a clean bowl, discard the seeds

Continues overleaf

Pistachio & raspberry vertical cake

continued

and weigh the purée – you need 175g. If it weighs too much, return the purée to the pan and continue to cook until reduced and the weight is correct. Leave to cool.

7 **Make the buttercream.** Using a balloon whisk, combine the sugar, egg whites and 1 tablespoon of water in a heatproof bowl. Set the bowl over a pan of gently simmering water and whisk continuously for 6 minutes, until the meringue is glossy, hot to the touch and leaves a thick ribbon trail when you lift the whisk.

8 Spoon the meringue into the bowl of a stand mixer fitted with the whisk, add the salt and whisk on medium speed for 5 minutes, until the meringue forms stiff, glossy peaks and cools to room temperature. Little by little, add the butter to the meringue mixture, whisking well between each addition and scraping down the inside of the bowl from time to time. Add the vanilla and mix again to combine. Fold in the cold raspberry purée with a rubber spatula until evenly incorporated.

9 **Assemble the cake.** Carefully unroll the cooled sponges and trim all the sides to neaten. Cut each sponge into two 30 x 10cm strips. Spread 4 tablespoons of the buttercream evenly over each sponge strip using a palette knife.

10 Starting with the first strip of sponge, roll it back up into a tight spiral. Place the roll at one end of the second strip with the ends touching and continue to roll so the first roll is inside the second strip of sponge. Repeat, adding the third and fourth sponge strips to make a large, squat Swiss roll.

11 Turn the rolled sponges so that they are flat-side down in the middle of a serving plate. Gently but firmly press the sponges together and chill for 15 minutes to firm up.

12 Reserve 6 tablespoons of the remaining buttercream and, using a palette knife, spread the rest smoothly over the top and sides of the cake, in an even layer. Spoon the reserved buttercream into the piping bag fitted with the star nozzle and pipe rosettes over the top and around the base of the cake, then chill the cake for 15 minutes.

13 To decorate, arrange raspberries and nibbed pistachios on top of the cake, and dot the base with more pistachio nibs to finish.

Cherry bakewell fondant fancies

Makes: 16
Hands on: 2 hours
  + overnight resting
Bake: 30 mins

FOR THE SPONGE
175g unsalted butter,
    cubed and softened
175g caster sugar
3 large eggs, lightly beaten
1 tsp vanilla paste
1 tsp almond extract
1 tsp finely grated unwaxed lemon zest
200g plain flour
2 tsp baking powder
pinch of salt
75g ground almonds
3 tbsp whole milk

FOR THE FILLING
250g frozen pitted cherries, defrosted
75g caster sugar
1½ tbsp lemon juice

FOR THE BUTTERCREAM
50g unsalted butter,
    cubed and softened
75g icing sugar, sifted,
    plus extra for dusting
½ tsp vanilla paste
1 tsp lemon juice

FOR THE COATING
150g mandelmassa (or marzipan,
    if you can't find mandelmassa)
500g fondant icing sugar, sifted
4 tbsp warm water
pink food-colouring paste

You will need
20cm square cake tin, greased,
    then lined (base and sides)
    with baking paper
small piping bag fitted with
    a medium open star nozzle
small piping bag fitted with
    a small writing nozzle

This 'fancy' sponge is flavoured with vanilla, lemon and a good helping of ground almonds. There's extra jam in the filling and a topping of mandelmassa, a Scandinavian almond paste that has a higher almond content than marzipan.

. . . .

1 **Make the sponge** (do this a day in advance of decorating). Heat the oven to 180°C/160°C fan/Gas 4. Beat the butter and sugar in a stand mixer fitted with a beater, on medium speed for 4 minutes, scraping down the inside of the bowl from time to time, until the mixture is pale and creamy. A little at a time, add the eggs, mixing well between each addition, then mix in the vanilla, almond extract and lemon zest.

2 Sift the flour, baking powder and salt into the bowl, add the ground almonds and milk and beat on low speed for 30 seconds, until smooth.

3 Spoon the mixture into the prepared tin, spread it level and bake on the middle shelf for 25–30 minutes, until well risen, golden, and a skewer inserted into the centre comes out clean. Leave the sponge to cool in the tin for 5–10 minutes, then turn it out onto a wire rack to cool completely. Once cold, cover and set aside until you're ready to decorate the next day.

4 **Make the filling.** Cook the cherries with the sugar and lemon juice in a small pan on a low–medium heat for 15 minutes, until the cherries are soft and jammy. Spoon them into a bowl and leave them to cool, then cover and set aside.

5 **Make the buttercream.** Beat the butter, icing sugar, vanilla and lemon juice until very pale and soft. Spoon the buttercream into the small piping bag fitted with the medium open star nozzle.

6 **Assemble the fondant fancies.** Trim the sides of the sponge to neaten, level the top, and cut it into 16 equal squares. Using a small, sharp knife, cut out a neat 1–2cm-deep cone in the middle of the top of each square, reserving the cones.

7 Spoon 1 teaspoon of the cherry jam into each hollow (you'll have some left over). Cut the flat end of each sponge cone into a disc to create a lid, then place it on top of the jam to cover.

8 **Coat the squares.** Lightly dust the work surface with icing sugar and roll out the mandelmassa into a 20cm square. Cut this into sixteen 5cm squares.

9 Lightly brush a little of the remaining cherry jam onto each mandelmassa square and place the squares on top of the cakes.

Continues overleaf

Cherry bakewell fondant fancies
continued

Turn the cakes upside down (mandelmassa on the work surface) and trim the sides of the mandelmassa to neaten. Turn the squares right way up and pipe a buttercream rosette on top of each. Loosely cover the cakes and chill for 1 hour, until firm.

10 Tip 450g of the fondant icing sugar into a large bowl. Whisking continuously, gradually add the warm water, 1 tablespoon at a time, until the icing is smooth and thick but pourable. Add the pink food-colouring paste, a drop at a time, and mix to combine to your desired shade.

11 Sit one cake on the tines of a fork. Hold the fork over the bowl and spoon the icing over the top and sides of the cake to cover. Using a palette knife, carefully slide the cake off the fork onto a wire rack. Repeat to ice all the cakes. Leave for 1 hour, until the icing sets.

12 Tip the remaining fondant icing sugar into a bowl. Whisk in enough water, 1 teaspoon at a time, until the icing is smooth and holds a ribbon trail. Spoon this into the piping bag fitted with the small writing nozzle and pipe delicate lines over the top of each cake, then leave to set before serving.

Layered lemon cake

Serves: 12
Hands on: 2 hours + chilling
Bake: 27 mins

FOR THE LEMON CURD
75g unsalted butter,
    cubed and softened
150g caster sugar
juice and finely grated zest
    of 3 unwaxed lemons
2 large eggs, lightly beaten
1 large egg yolk, lightly beaten

FOR THE LEMON SPONGES
380g unsalted butter,
    cubed and softened
380g caster sugar
6 large eggs, lightly beaten
finely grated zest of
    6 unwaxed lemons
380g self-raising flour, sifted
5 tbsp lemon juice (the juice
    of about 2 lemons)

FOR THE BUTTERCREAM
310g unsalted butter,
    cubed and softened
700g icing sugar, sifted
1 tsp vanilla extract
6 tbsp whole milk

FOR THE WHITE
CHOCOLATE GANACHE
300g white chocolate, chopped
100ml double cream

TO DECORATE
3 tbsp freeze-dried raspberries
a few blueberries and raspberries, or
    other seasonal fruit of your choice
your choice of edible flowers

You will need
20cm round cake tins x 3, greased,
    then base-lined with baking paper
medium piping bag fitted with a
    medium open star nozzle

Making this cake always makes me smile. It's a zesty zingy slice of lemon happiness all in one cake and a firm favourite with my family and friends. The edible fresh flowers and seasonal berries make for such a pretty decoration.

1 **Make the lemon curd.** Mix the butter, sugar and lemon juice and zest in a heatproof bowl. Set the bowl over a pan of gently simmering water and stir until the butter melts. Add the whole eggs and yolk and cook for 10 minutes, stirring continuously until the curd thickens enough to coat the back of the spoon. Strain the curd into a clean bowl, leave it to cool, then cover the surface with baking paper and chill for at least 2 hours, until ready to use.

2 **Make the lemon sponges.** Heat the oven to 180°C/160°C fan/ Gas 4. Beat the butter and caster sugar in a stand mixer fitted with the beater, on medium speed for 5 minutes, scraping down the inside of the bowl from time to time, until pale and creamy. A little at a time, add the eggs, beating well between each addition until mixed in.

3 Add the lemon zest with 2–3 tablespoons of the flour and mix on low speed to combine. Sift in the remaining flour in two batches and mix on low until combined. Mix in the lemon juice.

4 Divide the mixture equally between the prepared cake tins and spread it level using a palette knife or the back of a spoon. Then, gently tap the tins on the work surface to knock out any large air pockets.

5 Bake the sponges on the middle shelves for 25–27 minutes, until they are risen and golden, and a skewer inserted into the centres comes out clean. Leave them to cool in the tins for a few minutes, then turn them out onto a wire rack to cool completely. Using a cake leveller or long serrated knife, trim the domed top off each sponge. Set aside.

6 **Make the buttercream.** Beat the butter in a stand mixer fitted with the beater, on medium speed for 5 minutes, until pale and creamy. Scrape down the inside of the bowl, add half the icing sugar and mix on low speed until combined. Increase the mixer speed to medium and beat for 4 minutes, until pale and fluffy.

7 Add the remaining icing sugar and the vanilla and beat for a further 5 minutes. Scrape down the inside of the bowl again, then gradually add the milk, mixing until the buttercream is a spreadable consistency.

8 **Make the white chocolate ganache.** Melt the white chocolate with the cream in a heatproof bowl in the microwave for

Continues overleaf

Layered
lemon
cake
continued

30 seconds at a time, stirring between bursts, until melted. Leave it to cool for a few minutes, then chill for 15 minutes, until firmed up.

9 Using an electric hand whisk, whisk the white chocolate ganache for 2 minutes, until light and fluffy.

10 **Assemble the cake.** Place a little buttercream in the centre of a serving plate and top with the first sponge layer. Using a palette knife, spread the top of the sponge with 3–4 tablespoons of the buttercream. Take the second sponge layer and spread 2–3 tablespoons of the lemon curd on top. Turn the sponge over and place it, lemon curd-side down, on the first sponge layer. Repeat with the third sponge.

11 Using a palette knife, spread a thin layer of buttercream over the top and sides of the cake to crumb coat, then chill it for 30 minutes, until firm. Add 3–4 tablespoons of the lemon curd to the remaining buttercream for the top layer of icing. (You will have some lemon curd left over – you can store it in a jar in the fridge for up to 2 weeks and enjoy it on toast.)

12 Place the cake on an icing turntable and, using a cake scraper or palette knife, spread an even, smooth layer of the lemon buttercream around the sides and over the top of the cake, then chill the cake again for 15 minutes.

13 Fill the medium piping bag fitted with an open star nozzle with the white chocolate ganache and pipe rosettes onto the top of the cake in whichever way you fancy. Gently press the freeze-dried raspberries around the base of the cake, then dot the top of the cake with the blueberries and raspberries (or your choice of fruit) between the rosettes. Finish by interspersing the edible flowers.

Blueberry, pecan & cinnamon crumble traybake

Serves: 12
Hands on: 30 mins
Bake: 45 mins

FOR THE CRUMBLE
75g pecans, finely chopped
75g light brown soft sugar
50g plain flour
2 tsp ground cinnamon
25g unsalted butter, melted

FOR THE SPONGE
225g unsalted butter,
    cubed and softened
225g caster sugar
3 large eggs, lightly beaten
250g plain flour
2 tsp baking powder
½ tsp bicarbonate of soda
pinch of salt
3 tbsp soured cream
    or buttermilk
3 tbsp tahini
1 tsp vanilla paste
125g blueberries

You will need
30 x 20cm traybake tin, greased,
    then lined (base and sides)
    with baking paper

This crumble traybake is often known as coffee cake in the USA – not because it's coffee-flavoured, but simply because it's delicious with a morning brew. The addition of tahini gives the bake a delicately nutty flavour.

. . . .

1 **Make the crumble.** Heat the oven to 180°C/160°C fan/Gas 4. Mix the pecans, sugar, flour and cinnamon in a bowl. Add the melted butter and mix until combined and the mixture starts to clump together. Set aside.

2 **Make the sponge.** Beat the butter and sugar in a stand mixer fitted with the beater, on medium speed, for 4 minutes, scraping down the inside of the bowl from time to time, until the mixture is pale and creamy. A little at a time, add the eggs, mixing well between each addition.

3 Sift the flour, baking powder, bicarbonate of soda and salt into the bowl. Add the soured cream or buttermilk, and the tahini and vanilla, and mix again, on low speed, for 30 seconds, until smooth.

4 **Assemble the traybake.** Spoon two-thirds of the sponge mixture into the prepared tin and spread it level. Scatter half of the crumble over the top in an even layer.

5 Carefully spoon over the remaining sponge mixture, taking care not to disrupt the crumble layer below, and gently spread it level using an offset palette knife. Scatter with the blueberries, followed by the remaining crumble.

6 Bake the traybake on the middle shelf for 40–45 minutes, until risen and golden, and a skewer inserted into the centre comes out clean. Leave to cool in the tin and cut the traybake into 16 squares to serve.

Vanilla, almond & apricot celebration cake

You've heard of apricot and almond tart, but in this recipe those flavours are reinvented in a beautiful celebration cake that sings with almondiness and is coated in a stunning vintage-look buttercream with delicate, piped decoration.

. . . .

Serves: 16–20
Hands on: 2½ hours + chilling
Bake: 25 mins

FOR THE SPONGES
300g caster sugar
250g plain flour
3½ tsp baking powder
100g ground almonds
pinch of salt
6 eggs
120ml vegetable oil
100g full-fat natural yogurt
2 tsp vanilla paste
1½ tbsp almond extract
180g unsalted butter, melted

FOR THE APRICOT FILLING
250g dried apricots, halved
3 tbsp runny honey
2 vanilla pods, halved lengthways
    and seeds scraped out

FOR THE VANILLA BUTTERCREAM
6 large egg whites
400g caster sugar
600g unsalted butter,
    cubed and softened
1 tbsp vanilla paste
pale blue food-colouring gel
pale pink food-colouring gel

TO DECORATE
coloured sprinkles

You will need
20cm sandwich tins x 3, greased,
    then base-lined with baking paper
sugar thermometer
2 medium piping bags
3 small piping bags
3 piping nozzles: medium closed star;
    small writing; and small open star
25cm cake board
cake turntable

1 **Make the sponges.** Heat the oven to 170°C /150°C fan/ Gas 3. Sift the sugar, flour, baking powder, ground almonds and salt into a large bowl, mix until combined and set aside.

2 In a separate bowl, whisk together the eggs, vegetable oil, yogurt, vanilla paste and almond extract. Gradually, whisk the egg mixture into the dry ingredients until combined. Whisk in the melted butter to make a smooth, pourable mixture.

3 Divide the mixture equally between the prepared sandwich tins and spread it level with a palette knife. Bake the sponges on the middle shelves for 20–25 minutes, until risen and golden, and a skewer inserted into the centres comes out clean. Leave the sponges to cool in their tins for 10 minutes, then turn them out onto a wire rack to cool completely.

4 **Make the apricot filling.** While the sponges are baking, place the dried apricots in a small–medium pan with the honey and vanilla pods and seeds. Pour in 500ml of water to cover and bring to the boil over a high heat. Turn the heat down and simmer for 20 minutes, until the apricots are soft and plump, and the liquid has reduced to a runny syrup consistency. Strain the apricots over a bowl, discarding the vanilla pods and reserving the syrup. Set aside 50ml of the syrup for soaking the sponges.

5 Blitz the remaining syrup with two-thirds of the apricots to a smooth, fairly thick purée. Stir in the remaining third of apricots and set aside until ready to use.

6 **Make the vanilla buttercream.** Whisk the egg whites and sugar in a heatproof bowl set over a pan of gently simmering water until the sugar dissolves and the mixture reaches 71°C on the sugar thermometer. Transfer the egg-white mixture to the bowl of a stand mixer fitted with the whisk and whisk on medium–high speed for 10 minutes, until you have a fluffy meringue that has cooled completely.

7 With the mixer still running, gradually add the butter, ensuring each addition is mixed in before adding the next. Once the butter has been incorporated, scrape down the inside of the bowl, then whisk in the vanilla for a further 5 minutes, until you have a smooth, spreadable buttercream.

Continues overleaf

Vanilla, almond & apricot celebration cake
continued

8 Transfer 450g of the buttercream to a separate bowl and colour it pale blue with a few drops of blue food-colouring gel. Set aside.

9 Spoon 175g of the plain buttercream into a medium piping bag fitted with the medium closed star nozzle, and 75g into a small piping bag fitted with the small plain writing nozzle.

10 Use the rest of the plain buttercream to fill the other medium piping bag, then snip off the tip to give a 1cm-diameter hole.

11 **Assemble the cake.** Using a long, serrated knife level the top of each sponge if necessary. Using a pastry brush, brush each sponge layer with the reserved apricot syrup. Place the first sponge onto the cake board, then onto the cake turntable.

12 Using the medium piping bag with the 1cm-diameter hole, pipe a thin layer of buttercream over the top of the sponge and spread it to the edge using an offset spatula or palette knife. Over this, pipe a ring of buttercream around the outer edge, then spoon half of the apricot filling into the middle, spreading it out evenly to fill the ring of buttercream. Place the second sponge on top and repeat with the buttercream and apricot filling.

13 Place the last sponge on top and spread the remaining buttercream from the piping bag over the top and sides of the cake to create a thin crumb coat. Chill the cake for 20 minutes.

14 Using an offset spatula or palette knife, cover the top and sides of the chilled cake with a smooth layer of blue buttercream. Chill for a further 20 minutes.

15 Using a cocktail stick, lightly mark eight points, equally spaced apart, around the top edge of the cake. Taking the marks as a guide, use a small piping bag fitted with the small plain writing nozzle to pipe a semi-circle of plain buttercream between each mark, starting at the top and looping one-third of the way down the side of the cake and finishing again at the top.

16 From the medium piping bag fitted with the medium closed star nozzle, pipe swirls of plain buttercream around the base and top edge of the cake.

17 Colour any leftover plain buttercream pale pink using the food-colouring gel. Spoon three-quarters of the pink buttercream into a small piping bag fitted with the small open star nozzle, then pipe a small shell at the joins of each of the eight loops, and swirls of pink buttercream around the inside edge of the plain buttercream decoration on the top of the cake.

18 Spoon the remaining pink buttercream into a small piping bag fitted with the clean small plain writing nozzle and pipe dots of pink beneath the loops. Decorate the top with sprinkles.

Mini honey bundt cakes with baked figs

Makes: 12
Hands on: 40 mins
Bake: 17 mins

100g unsalted butter, cubed and
    softened, plus extra for greasing
75g caster sugar
75g runny orange blossom honey
    (or other flower variety)
2 eggs, lightly beaten
1 tsp finely grated unwaxed
    lemon zest
1 tsp finely grated unwaxed
    orange zest
175g plain flour
75g ground almonds
1½ tsp baking powder
½ tsp bicarbonate of soda
½ tsp ground cinnamon
½ tsp ground cardamom
pinch of salt
100g full-fat Greek-style yogurt,
    plus extra to serve

FOR THE BAKED FIGS
4 tbsp runny orange blossom honey
juice of ½ lemon
juice of ½ orange
1 cinnamon stick
6 figs, halved lengthways

You will need
large piping bag, fitted with a
    medium plain nozzle (optional)
12-hole mini bundt tin, greased
    and dusted with flour; or silicone
    moulds, greased
baking tray, lined with baking paper

Serve these sticky honey cakes while they are still warm, drizzled with citrus and honey syrup and with roasted figs and cool Greek yogurt. They would make a satisfying end to a late summer or early autumn dinner party.

. . . .

1 **Make the sponge.** Heat the oven to 180°C/160°C fan/Gas 4. Beat the butter, sugar and honey in a stand mixer fitted with the beater, on medium speed for 4 minutes, scraping down the inside of the bowl from time to time, until the mixture is pale and creamy. Add the eggs, a little at a time, mixing well between each addition, then add the lemon and orange zests and mix to combine.

2 Sift the flour, ground almonds, baking powder, bicarbonate of soda, cinnamon, cardamom and salt into the bowl. Add the yogurt and mix on low speed until smooth.

3 Spoon the mixture into the piping bag fitted with a medium plain nozzle and pipe or spoon the mixture into the prepared holes of the tin, filling them two-thirds full. It is easier and neater to fill the tin using a piping bag, but you can use a spoon instead, if you prefer.

4 Bake the sponges for 17 minutes, until risen, golden and a skewer inserted into each one comes out clean. Leave to cool in the tin for 1 minute, then carefully turn the bundts out onto a wire rack to cool slightly while you prepare the baked figs.

5 Increase the oven temperature to 200°C/180°C fan/Gas 6.

6 **Bake the figs.** Put the honey, lemon and orange juices and cinnamon stick in a small pan on a low–medium heat and bring the liquid to the boil. Reduce the heat slightly and simmer for 4 minutes, until reduced by half.

7 Arrange the figs, cut sides upwards, on the lined baking tray, drizzle each half with a little of the citrus-honey syrup (reserve the remainder to serve) and bake for 4–5 minutes, until soft and starting to caramelise at the edges.

8 Place one warm cake on each serving plate. Add a good spoonful of yogurt on the side, top with a fig half and drizzle everything with the remaining citrus-honey syrup.

Tiered coconut cake

This stunning tiered cake, fit for a wedding, uses both desiccated coconut and coconut cream to give the sponges an exceptional hit of coconut flavour. The cake is surrounded by white chocolate feathers, creating a delicate, beautiful collar.

Serves: 20
Hands on: 2 hours + chilling
Bake: 65 mins

FOR THE 20CM SPONGES
250g unsalted butter,
    cubed and softened
250g caster sugar
4 eggs, lightly beaten
2 tsp vanilla extract or paste
250g plain flour
3 tsp baking powder
pinch of salt
75g unsweetened desiccated coconut
4 tbsp coconut cream

FOR THE 15CM AND 10CM SPONGES
175g unsalted butter,
    cubed and softened
175g caster sugar
3 eggs, lightly beaten
1 tsp vanilla paste
175g plain flour
2 tsp baking powder
pinch of salt
50g desiccated coconut
3 tbsp coconut cream

FOR THE PASSION FRUIT CURD
6 yolks (save the whites
    for the frosting)
180g caster sugar
6 tbsp passion fruit purée
1 tbsp lime or yuzu juice
125g unsalted butter, cubed

FOR THE FROSTING
325g caster sugar
6 egg whites
pinch of salt
500g unsalted butter,
    cubed and softened
2 tsp vanilla paste
4 tbsp coconut cream

FOR THE VANILLA SYRUP
75g caster sugar
1 vanilla pod, seeds scraped out

Continues overleaf

1 **Make the 20cm sponges.** Heat the oven to 180°C/160°C fan/Gas 4. Beat the butter and sugar in a stand mixer fitted with the beater, on medium speed for 3–4 minutes, scraping down the bowl from time to time, until light and creamy. A little at a time, add the eggs, mixing well between each addition. Mix in the vanilla, then sift in the flour, baking powder and salt, add the desiccated coconut and coconut cream and beat until smooth.

2 Divide the mixture equally between the 20cm sandwich tins and spread it level. Bake on the middle shelves for 25–30 minutes, until risen and golden, and a skewer inserted into the centres comes out clean. Leave to cool in the tins for 5 minutes, then turn out the sponges onto a wire rack to cool completely.

3 Repeat steps 1 and 2 to make both the 15cm and the 10cm sponges, using 275g of the mixture for the smaller tin and the remainder for the larger. Bake the sponges for 30–35 minutes, until risen and golden, and a skewer inserted into the centres comes out clean. Leave the cakes to cool in the tins for 5 minutes, then carefully turn them out onto a wire rack to cool completely.

4 **Make the passion fruit curd.** While the cakes are baking and cooling, beat the egg yolks in a heatproof bowl. Add the remaining ingredients and set the bowl over a pan of gently simmering water (do not allow the bottom of the bowl to touch the water or the eggs will scramble) and heat, stirring continuously, for 15 minutes, until you have a very thick custard. Remove the bowl from the heat, strain the mixture into a clean bowl, cover the surface with a disc of baking paper and leave to cool. When cold, chill the curd for 2 hours, until firm and spreadable.

5 **Make the frosting.** While the curd is chilling, put the sugar, egg whites and salt in a large heatproof glass bowl set over a pan of gently simmering water. Add 1 tablespoon of water and whisk until the sugar dissolves and the mixture is foamy. Continue whisking continuously for 3 minutes, until the mixture is hot to the touch, increases in volume and leaves a thick ribbon trail when you lift the whisk. Pour it into the bowl of a stand mixer fitted with a whisk and beat on a medium–high speed for 5 minutes, until doubled in volume and thick, glossy and cold.

6 Gradually add the butter to the frosting mixture, beating until smooth. Mix in the vanilla and coconut cream to combine.

Continues overleaf

Tiered coconut cake
continued

TO DECORATE
350g good-quality white chocolate,
    chopped (for the feathers)
silk or edible flowers

You will need
20cm sandwich tins x 2, greased,
    then base-lined with baking paper
15cm round cake tin, greased, then
    base-lined with baking paper
10cm round cake tin, greased, then
    base-lined with baking paper
20cm, 15cm and 10cm cake boards
large piping bag fitted with
    a medium plain nozzle
2 baking sheets, lined with
    baking paper
8–10 cake dowel rods

7   **Make the vanilla syrup.** Tip the sugar into a small pan, add the seeds and 75ml of water and slowly bring the syrup to the boil to dissolve the sugar, swirling the pan occasionally. Leave to cool.

8   **Assemble the sponges.** Cut the 20cm sponges in half horizontally to give four 20cm layers. Place the bottom half of one of the sponge layers on the 20cm cake board and lightly brush with the vanilla syrup. Spoon one-quarter of the frosting into the piping bag and pipe a ring of frosting around the top edge of the sponge. Fill the middle of the ring with 2–3 tablespoons of the passion fruit curd. Repeat this filling and layering for two more sponges, ending with the fourth 20cm sponge layer. Chill for 20 minutes, until firm.

9   Meanwhile, cut the 15cm and 10cm sponges each horizontally into three layers, then place them on the equivalent cake boards and fill and stack them as for the 20cm cake, refilling the piping bag with more frosting as needed but leaving about one-third to cover the cake. Chill for 20 minutes, until firm, then use a palette knife to spread a thin layer of frosting over the top and sides of each cake to crumb coat. Chill for another 20 minutes, until firm.

10   Cover the top and sides of each cake with the remaining frosting, spreading it smoothly and evenly with a palette knife. Chill for 30 minutes, until firm.

11   **Make the chocolate feathers.** Meanwhile, melt the white chocolate in a heatproof bowl set over a pan of gently simmering water. Stir until smooth and remove from the heat. Spoon ten 3cm discs of the melted chocolate onto the lined baking sheets, spaced well apart. Using a pastry brush or the back of a spoon, spread the chocolate discs into a feather shape – they can be slightly different in size but should be taller than the height of each cake. Chill for 15 minutes, until set, then carefully lift the feathers off the paper with a palette knife and transfer them to another lined sheet to chill. Set aside 2 tablespoons of the melted chocolate and repeat to make about 50–60 feathers in total.

12   **Decorate the cakes.** Brush a blob of the reserved melted chocolate (reheat if needed) on the underside of each feather and press them upright around the sides of each cake to cover.

13   **Assemble the cake.** Place the 20cm cake on a serving plate. Cut 4–6 dowel rods to the same height as the cake and press them into the sponges, reaching to the plate and flush with the top of the cake, evenly spaced apart, to support the next cake layer.

14   Cut 4 dowel rods to the same height as the 15cm cake and press them into the sponges, evenly spaced apart. Place the 15cm cake on top of the 20cm cake. Place the 10cm cake on top. Decorate with silk or edible flowers of choice to finish.

Paul's caterpillar cake

Serves: 8–10
Hands on: 1 hour
Bake: 1 hour

FOR THE SPONGE
5 large eggs
125g caster sugar, plus
  extra for sprinkling
80g plain flour
50g cocoa powder

FOR THE MERINGUE DECORATIONS
2 large egg whites
100g caster sugar
green food-colouring paste
red food-colouring paste
yellow food-colouring paste

FOR THE GANACHE COATING
200g 54% dark chocolate, chopped
15g unsalted butter
300ml double cream

FOR THE CATERPILLAR FACE
75g white chocolate
50g icing sugar, sifted
black food-colouring paste
cornflour, for dusting
10g red fondant
10g white fondant

FOR THE CHOCOLATE FILLING
200g unsalted butter,
  cubed and softened
200g icing sugar, sifted
2 tbsp cocoa powder, sifted

You will need
33 x 23cm Swiss roll tin, greased,
  then lined (base and sides)
  with baking paper
3 small piping bags, each fitted
  with a small star nozzle
baking sheet, lined with baking paper
7cm round cutter or ring lined
  with acetate
small flat plate, lined with a disc
  of baking paper
small piping bag fitted with
  a small plain writing nozzle

Hooray! A caterpillar cake has come crawling into *The Great British Bake Off*! There are no ugly bugs at this ball! This is a chocolate Swiss roll evolved into a gorgeous birthday treat... The question is: what will you call yours?

1 **Make the sponge.** Heat the oven to 220°C/200°C fan/Gas 7. Whisk the eggs and sugar in a stand mixer fitted with the whisk, on high speed for 2–3 minutes, until it is pale, thick and leaves a ribbon trail. Sift the flour and cocoa powder into the bowl and gently fold it in using a large metal spoon, taking care not to beat any of the air out of the mixture, until combined.

2 Pour the mixture into the prepared tin and spread it evenly into the corners with a palette knife. Bake the sponge on the middle shelf for 10–12 minutes, until it is well risen, firm to the touch, and starts to shrink away from the sides of the tin. Remove from the oven and reduce the temperature to 120°C/100°C fan/Gas ¾.

3 Place a sheet of baking paper larger than the Swiss roll tin on the work surface and sprinkle with caster sugar. Carefully invert the cake onto the paper and remove the lining paper. Score a line 2cm in from the edge of one of the short sides, making sure you don't cut all the way through the sponge. Starting from the scored short side, tightly roll up the sponge using the paper to help, then transfer it to a wire rack to cool completely.

4 **Make the meringue decorations.** Whisk the egg whites in a stand mixer fitted with a whisk, to soft peaks. A spoonful at a time, add the sugar, whisking to incorporate, then continue to whisk until the meringue is stiff and glossy.

5 Place half of the meringue in a bowl, add a few drops of green food colouring and fold it in with a metal spoon to an even colour. Divide the remaining meringue between two bowls and colour one batch red and the other yellow. Spoon each coloured meringue into a small piping bag fitted with a small star nozzle. (If you have only one nozzle, then work with one colour at a time, washing the nozzle in between.)

6 Using the red, yellow and green meringue, pipe 7 small meringue kisses of each colour, about the size of a hazelnut, onto the lined baking sheet. Using the green meringue, pipe six legs in an 'L' shape, measuring about 2 x 4cm, and six legs in a reverse 'L' shape. Pipe two green curved antennae, each about 4cm long, then use the remaining meringue to pipe flowers to decorate the serving plate or board. Bake the decorations for 45 minutes, until dry. Remove from the oven and leave to cool on the baking sheet.

Continues overleaf

Paul's caterpillar cake

continued

7 **Make the ganache coating.** Put the chocolate and butter in a heatproof bowl and set aside. Pour the cream into a pan and slowly bring it just to the boil. Pour it into the bowl with the chocolate and butter and leave the hot cream to melt them slightly for 1 minute, then stir until smooth and glossy. Leave the ganache to cool and thicken before using.

8 **Prepare the caterpillar face.** Melt the white chocolate in a heatproof bowl set over a pan of gently simmering water, stirring until smooth. Place the 7cm cutter in the middle of the lined plate and pour in the melted chocolate, then leave it to cool and set.

9 **Make the chocolate filling.** Beat the butter, icing sugar and cocoa powder in a stand mixer fitted with the beater, on low speed for 1 minute, until combined. Increase the speed to high and beat for a further 3 minutes, until pale, creamy and smooth.

10 **Assemble the caterpillar.** Unroll the cooled Swiss roll and remove the baking paper. With one of the short sides facing you, make thirteen vertical cuts, 1.5cm apart and 15cm long into the sponge, so you now have fourteen strips of sponge that look like the keys on a piano. Cut the top of each alternate strip to remove seven sponge fingers (blitz or crumble these to make 'soil').

11 Spread the filling over the sponge and re-roll the Swiss roll tightly from the other (non-cut) short end (the strips will make the ridges on the caterpillar body). Transfer the sponge to a wire rack set over a sheet of baking paper. Carefully pour the thickened ganache over the sponge roll to coat it smoothly, then gently transfer it to a serving plate or board. Arrange the coloured meringue kisses on the ridges of the caterpillar's body, then set the legs and antennae in place.

12 **Decorate the face.** Mix the icing sugar with a few drops of water and the black food-colouring paste to make a thick icing, then spoon it into the small piping bag fitted with the writing nozzle. Remove the set white chocolate disc from the mould.

13 Dust the work surface with cornflour and roll out the red and white fondants until 3mm thick. Cut out two white ovals for the eyes and roll two tiny white balls for the pupils. Using the red fondant, cut out two circles for the cheeks and a small tongue shape. Dampen the back of the fondant eyes with a little water and press them in place on the white-chocolate face. Using the black icing, pipe an iris onto each eye, then pipe a mouth. Dampen the fondant cheeks and tongue and stick them in place on the face. Press a white fondant ball onto each iris.

14 Press the caterpillar face onto the thick end of the Swiss roll – the ganache will help it stay in place. Arrange the meringue flowers and chocolate soil on the serving plate or board, to finish.

2
Biscuits

Ginger crunch ice-cream sandwiches

Makes: 12
Hands on: 40 mins + chilling
    and overnight freezing
Bake: 13 mins

FOR THE ICE CREAM
250ml whole milk
375ml double cream
3 large egg yolks
75g light brown soft sugar
75g caster sugar
1 tsp vanilla paste
pinch of salt
130g speculoos spread

FOR THE COOKIES
100g unsalted butter, softened
150g caster sugar
75g golden syrup
25g black treacle
40g speculoos spread
1 egg
200g plain flour
½ tsp cream of tartar
½ tsp bicarbonate of soda
3 tsp ground ginger
1 tsp ground cinnamon
pinch of salt

You will need
2 large baking sheets,
    lined with baking paper
ice-cream machine
30 x 20cm plastic freezer box or
    baking tin, lined (base and sides)
    with baking paper
6cm plain round cutter

No run-of-the-mill wafers here! Spiced ginger biscuits form a crunchy surround for creamy speculoos ice cream.

. . . .

1 **Make the ice cream.** Pour the milk and half the cream into a pan and bring it to just below boiling point. Meanwhile, whisk the egg yolks, both types of sugar, and the vanilla and salt with a balloon whisk, until smooth and light. Pour the hot milk mixture into the egg-yolk mixture, whisking continuously until smooth.

2 Return the custard to the pan and cook on a low heat, stirring continuously, for 3 minutes, until the mixture thickens enough to coat the back of a spoon – do not let it boil or the eggs will scramble. Strain the custard into a clean bowl, add the remaining cream and the speculoos spread and whisk to combine into a silky custard. Cover and leave to cool, then chill for 2 hours.

3 **Make the cookies.** While the ice-cream mixture is chilling, beat the butter with 50g of the caster sugar in a stand mixer fitted with the beater, on medium speed for 30 seconds to combine. Add the golden syrup, treacle and speculoos spread and beat again for 3–4 minutes, until soft and creamy, scraping down the inside of the bowl from time to time. Add the egg and mix again until combined. Sift in the flour, cream of tartar, bicarbonate of soda, 2 teaspoons of the ground ginger, ½ teaspoon of the ground cinnamon and the pinch of salt and mix on low until smooth. Cover and chill for 1 hour, until the mixture has firmed up a little.

4 Heat the oven to 180°C/160°C fan/Gas 4. Mix the remaining sugar and spices together in a tray. Roll the cookie dough into 30 cherry-tomato-sized balls and coat each one in the spiced sugar.

5 Arrange the cookie balls on the lined baking trays, leaving space between each one to allow for spreading. Flatten the top of each ball with a fork in a criss-cross pattern and bake for 12–13 minutes, until golden brown. The edge of the cookies should be crisp, and the middle still slightly soft – they will crisp further on cooling. Leave the cookies on the trays for 5 minutes, then transfer them to a wire rack to cool completely.

6 **Finish the ice cream.** Churn the chilled custard mixture in an ice-cream machine following the manufacturer's instructions until soft set. Crush six ginger cookies into rubbly crumbs. Spoon the ice cream into the lined freezer box or tin, lightly stir in the cookie crumbs and spread the ice cream smooth – it should be 2–3cm deep. Cover and freeze it overnight or until ready to serve.

7 **Assemble the ice-cream sandwiches.** Using the cutter, stamp out 12 discs of ice cream and sandwich each one between two cookies. If you're not serving the sandwiches right away, store them for up to 3 days in an airtight box in the freezer.

Iced party rings

Makes: 20
Hands on: 30 mins
  + chilling and setting
Bake: 12 mins

FOR THE BISCUITS
125g unsalted butter,
    cubed and softened
125g caster sugar
1 tsp vanilla extract
1 egg, lightly beaten
200g plain flour
30g cornflour
1 tbsp malted milk powder
½ tsp baking powder
pinch of salt

FOR THE ICING
500g icing sugar, sifted,
    plus extra if needed
1 egg white
at least 3 different colours
    of food-colouring paste
    (use your favourites)

You will need
7cm and 2cm fluted cookie cutters
2 baking sheets, lined with
    baking paper
small wooden skewers
    or cocktail sticks
at least 4 small piping bags,
    each fitted with a small
    writing nozzle

Iced party rings are given the retro tie-dye treatment to create an altogether modern take on this favourite treat.

· · · · · · · · · · · · ·

1 **Make the biscuits.** Beat the butter, sugar and vanilla in a stand mixer fitted with the beater, on medium speed for 3–5 minutes, scraping down the inside of the bowl from time to time, until pale and creamy. Mix in the egg until incorporated. Sift in the flour, cornflour, milk powder, baking powder and salt and mix on low speed for 30 seconds, until just combined. Shape the dough into a ball, then flatten it into a disc, and wrap and chill it for 2 hours, until firm.

2 Lightly flour the work surface and roll out the dough to about 3mm thick. Using the 7cm cutter, stamp out biscuit rounds and arrange them on the lined baking sheets, leaving a little space between each one. Using the 2cm cutter, stamp out circles from the middle of each round. Gather the dough offcuts into a ball, then re-roll and stamp out more 7cm rounds, and stamp out the centres, to make about 20 biscuits in total. Chill the biscuits for 30 minutes, while you heat the oven to 180°C/160°C fan/Gas 4.

3 Bake the biscuits for 12 minutes, until the edges are lightly golden. Leave them to cool and firm up on the baking sheets for 5 minutes before transferring to a wire rack to cool completely.

4 **Make the icing.** While the biscuits are cooling, using a balloon whisk, beat the icing sugar with the egg white and 3 tablespoons of water in a large bowl for 2 minutes, until the icing is smooth and holds a ribbon trail for 5 seconds when you lift the whisk. You may need more water or icing sugar for the right consistency.

5 Divide the icing equally between four or more bowls (one per colour, and one for the white). Tint three or more of the bowls of icing using the food-colouring pastes, adding it gradually on the point of a wooden skewer to your desired shade. Leave the icing in the remaining bowl white. Spoon 2 tablespoons of each icing into a small piping bag fitted with a small writing nozzle.

6 **Decorate the biscuits.** Two biscuits at time, dip the top of each one into your chosen bowl of icing to coat evenly, allowing any excess to drip back into the bowl, then place the biscuits back on the cooling rack. Pipe fine lines or concentric circles around the top of each biscuit in contrasting colours, then, working quickly, drag a clean wooden skewer or cocktail stick through the icing in alternate directions to create a feather pattern. Continue to decorate the rest of the biscuits, two at a time, then leave the icing to set for 2 hours before serving. The biscuits will keep in an airtight box for up to 2–3 days.

White chocolate, pistachio & cranberry shortbreads

Makes: 32
Hands on: 40 mins + chilling
Bake: 25 mins

125g unsalted pistachios
225g unsalted butter,
    cubed and softened
115g granulated sugar
¼ tsp salt
340g plain flour
100g dried cranberries,
    chopped into small pieces
100g white chocolate, chopped
    into 5mm–1cm pieces

TO DECORATE
180g white chocolate, chopped
25g pistachios, finely chopped

You will need
2 large baking sheets,
    lined with baking paper
5.5cm plain round cutter

**This recipe is a firm family favourite –
my mum especially loves the combination
of sweet with nutty. I remember reaching
for the shortbreads as a cheeky little boy
and being warned not to spoil my dinner!**

1 **Toast the pistachios.** Heat the oven to 190°C/170°C fan/Gas 5. Tip the pistachios into a baking tray and toast them in the oven for 4–5 minutes, until slightly golden. Turn the oven off for the time being. Leave the pistachios to cool, then roughly chop.

2 **Make the dough.** Beat the butter, sugar and salt in a stand mixer fitted with the beater, on medium speed for 3–4 minutes, scraping down the inside of the bowl from time to time, until smooth and creamy.

3 Sift in the flour and mix on a low speed until just incorporated. Increase the speed to medium and mix for a further 30 seconds, until the dough just starts to come together. Add the pistachios, cranberries and white chocolate and mix on low speed until thoroughly combined and the mixture clumps together.

4 Tip the dough onto a large sheet of baking paper and place another sheet on top. Using your hands, flatten the dough into a disc, then switch to a rolling pin and roll the dough until it is 1cm thick.

5 **Stamp out the shortbreads.** Peel off the top sheet of baking paper and, using the cutter, stamp out as many shortbread discs as you can. Place the discs on the lined baking sheets, leaving space between each one to allow for spreading during baking. Gather the offcuts into a ball, re-roll and stamp out more discs – you should get about 32 in total. Prick the shortbreads with a fork and chill for 20 minutes to firm up. Meanwhile, heat the oven to 170°C/150°C fan/Gas 3.

6 **Bake the shortbreads.** Transfer the baking sheets to the oven and bake the shortbreads for 20–25 minutes, until light golden. Leave to cool on the tray for 2 minutes, then transfer them to a wire rack to cool completely.

7 **Decorate the shortbreads.** Melt the white chocolate in a heatproof bowl either in the microwave in 30-second bursts or over a pan of gently simmering water. Stir the chocolate until smooth and remove from the heat. Dip half of each cooled shortbread into the melted chocolate to coat. Place on a clean sheet of baking paper, scatter the chopped pistachios over the chocolate and leave to set before serving. The shortbreads will store for up to 3 days in an airtight box.

Florentine cookies

These hybrid florentines combine crisp, buttery biscuits with a fruity, chewy caramel top.

Makes: 24
Hands on: 30 mins
  + chilling and cooling
Bake: 21 mins

FOR THE COOKIES
150g unsalted butter,
    cubed and softened
125g icing sugar, sifted
2 tsp finely grated
    unwaxed orange zest
1 tsp vanilla paste
1 egg, lightly beaten
1 egg yolk
1 tbsp orange juice
225g plain flour
100g cornflour
½ tsp baking powder
pinch of salt

FOR THE TOPPING
100g glacé cherries, rinsed,
    patted dry and quartered
2 balls of stem ginger in syrup,
    drained, then finely chopped
75g mixed candied peel
75g flaked almonds
50g nibbed unsalted pistachios
1 tbsp plain flour
½ tsp ground ginger
pinch of salt
100g unsalted butter, cubed
100g demerara sugar
3 tbsp whole milk
2 tbsp runny honey

TO DECORATE
200g 70% dark chocolate, chopped
50g white chocolate, chopped

You will need
2 large baking sheets,
    lined with baking paper
6cm plain cutter
2 small piping bags, each fitted
    with a small writing nozzle

1 **Make the cookies.** Beat the butter and icing sugar in a stand mixer fitted with the beater, on medium speed for 3–5 minutes, scraping down the inside of the bowl from time to time, until pale and creamy. Mix in the orange zest and vanilla paste. A little at a time, add the whole egg and yolk, beating between each addition, until just combined. Add the orange juice and mix again.

2 Sift the flour, cornflour, baking powder and salt into the bowl and mix again briefly on low speed until just combined – do not over-beat the mixture. Shape the dough into a ball, then flatten it into a disc, and wrap and chill it for 2 hours, until firm.

3 Lightly dust the work surface with flour and roll out the dough to about 3–4mm thick. Using the cutter, stamp out rounds, arranging them on the baking sheets with a little space between each biscuit. Re-roll the offcuts and stamp out more rounds to make 24 cookies in total. Chill them for 20 minutes while you make the topping and heat the oven to 180°C/160°C fan/Gas 4.

4 **Make the topping.** Mix the cherries with the stem ginger, peel, almonds, pistachios, flour, ground ginger and salt. Set aside.

5 Heat the butter, sugar, milk and honey in a pan on a low heat, stirring to melt the butter. Bring to a boil, then pour the mixture into the bowl with the fruit and nuts and combine. Leave to cool.

6 **Bake the cookies.** When the cookies have chilled, bake them for 8 minutes, until pale and just firm. Leave to cool for 10 minutes on the baking sheets, then divide the fruit-and-nut mixture between the cookies, spooning it on top. Return the cookies to the oven and bake them for a further 12–13 minutes, until golden and bubbling. Leave to cool slightly, then place the cookies on a clean lined baking sheet and leave until cold.

7 **Decorate the florentines.** Melt the dark chocolate in a heatproof bowl set over a pan of gently simmering water. Remove from the heat and stir until smooth. Dip the underside of each biscuit in the melted chocolate, shaking off any excess, then place them chocolate-side down on the clean sheet of baking paper. Spoon any leftover melted chocolate into a piping bag fitted with a small writing nozzle.

8 Melt the white chocolate, then spoon it into the second small piping bag. Drizzle the melted white and remaining dark chocolate over the top of each cookie and leave to set. The cookies will store for up to 3 days in an airtight box.

Prue's custard creams

Makes: 12
Hands on: 1 hour + chilling
Bake: 15 mins

FOR THE BISCUITS
100g unsalted butter,
   cubed and softened
100g caster sugar
1 egg
½ tsp vanilla extract
175g plain flour
35g custard powder

FOR THE CRÈME AU BEURRE
65g caster sugar
2 egg yolks
20g custard powder
150g unsalted butter,
   cubed and softened

You will need
custard cream biscuit
   cutter and stamp
2 baking sheets, lined
   with baking paper
sugar thermometer
medium piping bag fitted
   with a medium plain nozzle

Thought to have first appeared in the 1900s, the custard cream is arguably Britain's most iconic biscuit. Baking your own, with a silky cream filling, takes our favourite teatime treat to a whole new level of moreish dunk-ability.

. . . .

1 **Make the biscuits.** Beat the butter and sugar in a stand mixer fitted with the beater, on medium speed for 2–3 minutes, until light and creamy. Add the egg and vanilla and thoroughly mix.

2 Sift in the flour and custard powder and mix by hand to a crumbly dough. Bring the dough together with your hands and knead it gently on a lightly floured work surface until smooth. Do not overwork the biscuit dough.

3 Divide the dough in half and shape each half into a flat disc, then wrap and chill them for 1 hour.

4 Roll out one of the discs of dough on a lightly floured work surface until about 3mm thick. Lightly flour the custard cream biscuit cutter and stamp, then cut out and stamp 12 biscuits, flouring the cutter and stamp each time.

5 Place the biscuits on one of the lined baking sheets and chill them while you roll out the remaining dough to make 12 more custard cream biscuits. Chill the biscuits for 30 minutes and heat the oven to 170°C/150°C fan/Gas 3.

6 Bake the biscuits for 12–14 minutes, until the edges start to turn a golden colour. Leave them to cool on the baking sheets for 5 minutes, then transfer them to a wire rack to cool completely.

7 **Make the crème au beurre.** Tip the sugar into a small pan, add 2 tablespoons of water and bring it to the boil. Boil the mixture until the temperature on the sugar thermometer reaches 115°C.

8 Put the egg yolks in the bowl of stand mixer fitted with a whisk and whisk on low speed. Slowly and carefully pour the hot sugar syrup over the egg yolks, then increase the speed to high and whisk until the mixture is thick and leaves a ribbon trail when you lift the whisk. Sift the custard powder over the surface of the mixture and whisk again until the mixture is cool to the touch.

9 A little at a time, gradually add the butter, whisking continuously until incorporated. Spoon the crème au beurre into the piping bag fitted with the medium plain nozzle and chill it until you're ready to assemble the biscuits.

10 **Assemble the custard creams.** Turn 12 of the biscuits design-side down and pipe equal amounts of the crème au beurre around the edges and in the middle of each one. Sandwich with the remaining 12 biscuits, design-side out, on top, then chill the biscuits until the filling is firm. They will keep for up to 3 days in an airtight box.

Choc-chip cookies

My ultimate chocolate chip cookies are my all-time favourite comfort food. Not only are they great to snack on, but I also love them warmed up and then topped with ice cream and caramel sauce. Perfect mouthfuls!

Makes: 30–36
Hands on: 20 mins + chilling
Bake: 15 mins

240g unsalted butter,
   cubed and softened
150g caster sugar
180g light brown soft sugar
2 tsp vanilla extract
2 eggs, lightly beaten
400g plain flour
1 tsp bicarbonate of soda
1 tsp baking powder
pinch of salt
340g 70% dark chocolate,
   chopped into 1cm pieces
2 tsp lightly crushed sea-salt
   flakes, for sprinkling

You will need
2 baking sheets, greased,
   then lined with baking paper

1 **Make the cookie dough.** Beat the butter with both types of sugar and the vanilla in a stand mixer fitted with the beater, on medium speed for 3 minutes, scraping down the inside of the bowl from time to time, until light and creamy. One at a time, add the eggs, and mix well until combined.

2 Sift the flour, bicarbonate of soda, baking powder and salt into the bowl and mix until almost combined. Mix in the chocolate until thoroughly combined.

3 **Shape the cookies.** Scoop the cookie dough into 30–36 equal-sized balls, about 50g each, and place them on the lined baking sheets, leaving space between each one to allow for spreading during cooking. Chill the cookies for 1 hour to firm up.

4 **Bake the cookies.** Heat the oven to 190°C/170°C fan/Gas 5. Bake the cookies for 12–14 minutes, until pale and golden. Scatter a small pinch of sea-salt flakes over the top of each one and leave them to cool on the baking sheets for 2 minutes. Transfer the cookies to a wire rack to cool completely. The cookies will store for up to 3 days in an airtight box.

Pecorino, walnut & rosemary shortbreads

Makes: 36
Hands on: 20 mins + chilling
Bake: 20 mins

FOR THE SHORTBREAD DOUGH
125g plain flour
75g spelt flour
pinch of cayenne
125g unsalted butter,
    cubed and chilled
100g pecorino, finely grated
50g walnuts, toasted and
    finely chopped
1 tbsp finely chopped rosemary
    or sage leaves
1 egg, separated
1 tbsp chilled water
salt and freshly ground
    black pepper

TO DECORATE
50g walnuts, very finely chopped
1 tbsp sesame seeds
1 tbsp black sesame seeds
    or black onion seeds

You will need
large baking sheet, lined
    with baking paper

Shortbreads – but probably not as you know them. These savoury nibbles are the perfect salty snack served with a pre-dinner drink – a blonde beer, a prosecco, a G&T or an elderflower spritz would match perfectly.

. . . .

1 **Make the shortbread dough.** Sift both flours into a large bowl, add the cayenne and season well with salt and pepper. Rub in the butter with your fingertips until the mixture resembles breadcrumbs, then mix in the pecorino, walnuts and herbs until combined.

2 Make a well in the centre, add the egg yolk and the chilled water and mix with a table knife. When the mixture starts to clump, use your hands to bring the dough together into a ball and knead it very gently until smooth.

3 Turn out the dough onto a very lightly floured work surface or board. Shape the dough into a neat 38cm log, wrap the log in baking paper and chill for 2 hours, until very firm.

4 **Shape and decorate the shortbreads.** Heat the oven to 180°C/160°C fan/Gas 4. On a plate, mix the walnuts for decoration with the seeds.

5 Unwrap the dough log, brush it with the egg white and roll it in the nut and seed mixture until evenly coated. Cut the log into 1cm-thick slices (about 36 in total), and arrange these flat on the lined baking sheet.

6 **Bake the shortbreads.** Transfer the baking sheet to the oven and bake the shortbreads for 20 minutes, until firm and starting to turn golden. Leave them to cool on the baking sheet – they will firm up further as they cool. The shortbreads will store for up to 3 days in an airtight box.

Cosmic Neapolitan bites

These tricolour cookies wouldn't be out of place at a 70s themed party. The combo of vanilla, raspberry and chocolate doughs not only brings swirly colour, but delicious Neapolitan flavours, too. And no two cookies are the same.

. . . .

Makes: 28
Hands on: 1 hour + chilling
Bake: 14 mins

FOR THE VANILLA DOUGH
125g butter, cubed and softened
125g caster sugar
1 tsp vanilla paste
1 egg yolk
200g plain flour
25g cornflour
½ tsp baking powder
pinch of salt
1 tbsp whole milk

FOR THE RASPBERRY DOUGH
125g butter, cubed and softened
125g caster sugar
1 egg yolk
2 tbsp freeze-dried raspberry powder
pink food-colouring paste
200g plain flour
25g cornflour
½ tsp baking powder
pinch of salt
2 tsp whole milk

FOR THE CHOCOLATE DOUGH
125g butter, cubed and softened
125g caster sugar
1 egg yolk
1 tbsp whole milk
150g plain flour
35g cocoa powder
25g cornflour
½ tsp baking powder
pinch of salt

You will need
2 large baking sheets,
   lined with baking paper

1 **Make the vanilla dough.** Beat the butter, sugar and vanilla paste in a stand mixer fitted with the beater, on medium speed for 3–4 minutes, scraping down the inside of the bowl from time to time, until pale and creamy. Add the egg yolk and mix again until combined.

2 Sift the flour, cornflour, baking powder and salt into the bowl, add the milk and mix on low until just combined – do not overmix the dough. Turn out the dough onto the work surface and knead it gently into a ball, flatten it into a rectangle, then cover and chill.

3 **Make the raspberry and chocolate doughs.** Repeat steps 1 and 2 to make the raspberry dough, adding the freeze-dried raspberry powder and a drop or two of pink food-colouring paste after the egg yolk. Repeat again to make the chocolate dough, sifting in the cocoa powder with the flour. Chill the cookie doughs for about 2 hours, until firm.

4 **Assemble the cookies.** Cut each flavour of dough into four equal pieces. Take one piece of the vanilla dough and use your hands to roll it into a 25–30cm-long rope. Repeat with one piece of the raspberry dough and one piece of the chocolate dough.

5 Cut each rope in half to make six shorter pieces. Lay one piece of the vanilla, raspberry and chocolate rope on the work surface side-by-side, then top with three more pieces in the following order: chocolate, vanilla, raspberry. (You want the colours mixed up and not stacked on top of one another.)

6 Using your hands, roll the stacked dough pieces on the work surface to form a neat log, making sure there are no air pockets or spaces between the different-coloured strips of dough. Press the ends together to seal, then wrap the log tightly in baking paper and twist the ends to seal. Chill for 4 hours, until firm. Repeat with the remaining cookie dough to make 4 tightly wrapped multi-coloured dough logs.

7 **Bake the cookies.** Heat the oven to 180°C/160°C fan/Gas 4. Cut the logs into 1cm thick slices and arrange the slices on the lined baking sheets, leaving space between each cookie. Bake for 12–14 minutes, until firm and starting to turn golden at the edges. Leave to cool on the baking sheets. The cookies will store for up to 3 days in an airtight box.

Fruit, nut & seed flapjacks

Makes: 20
Hands on: 30 mins
Bake: 25 mins

75g toasted flaked almonds
350g porridge oats
75g unsweetened desiccated coconut
75g pumpkin seeds
1 tsp ground ginger
10g freeze-dried raspberry pieces
pinch of salt
100g soft dried apricots,
   chopped into 1cm pieces
175g unsalted butter, diced
225g golden syrup
200g light brown soft sugar

FOR THE TOPPING
200g blonde chocolate, chopped
oil-based pink food-colouring gel
2 tsp freeze-dried raspberry pieces

You will need
30 x 20cm brownie tin, greased,
   then lined (base and sides)
   with baking paper

These sophisticated flapjacks – packed with nuts, seeds and fruit, as well as the obligatory oats – are topped with caramelly, blonde chocolate. An oil-based food colouring prevents the chocolate from 'seizing', and gives a cleaner, brighter colour for swirling.

. . . .

1 **Make the flapjacks.** Heat the oven to 180°C/160°C fan/ Gas 4. In a large bowl, combine the flaked almonds, oats, coconut, pumpkin seeds, ground ginger, raspberry pieces and salt. Set aside.

2 Add the apricots to a pan with the butter, golden syrup and light brown soft sugar and place over a low–medium heat, stirring continuously, until the butter has melted and the sugar has dissolved. When the mixture starts to bubble, pour it into the bowl with the dry ingredients and mix to thoroughly combine.

3 Spoon the flapjack mixture into the prepared tin and level the top with the back of a spoon. Bake for 25 minutes, until golden brown, then leave the flapjack to cool and firm up in the tin.

4 **Make the topping.** Meanwhile, melt the blonde chocolate in a heatproof bowl set over a pan of gently simmering water. Stir the chocolate until smooth and remove the bowl from the heat. Spoon 1 tablespoon of the melted chocolate into a small bowl, add a drop of food colouring and mix until you have an even pink colour.

5 Pour the remaining melted blonde chocolate over the top of the cooled flapjack and spread it level with an offset palette knife. Drizzle the pink chocolate over the top and use the palette knife to swirl the two together.

6 Crush the raspberry pieces in a mortar with a pestle, or use the end of a rolling pin, until you have a powder, and scatter these over the top of the flapjack. Leave the chocolate at room temperature to set firm. Using a warmed knife, cut the flapjack into 20 squares or bars, ready to enjoy. They will store for up to a week in an airtight box.

3
Bread

Porridge bread

Makes: 1 loaf
Hands on: 25 mins + rising
Bake: 50 mins

FOR THE PORRIDGE
75g mixed grain rolled flakes
   for porridge (rolled oats, spelt
   and rye are a good combination),
   plus 50g extra for dusting
75ml whole milk

FOR THE DOUGH
400g strong white bread flour
4g fast-action dried yeast
2 tsp runny honey
2 tsp salt

You will need
proving basket or large bowl
   lined with a tea towel;
   or proving bag
baker's cloche or lidded
   cast-iron casserole
baking sheet, lined with a
   20cm disc of baking paper

The porridge for this bread calls for a mixture of grains to give the loaf extra-special texture and flavour. But, whatever porridge you're having for breakfast, never throw away your leftovers: with just 150g, you can skip the first step and turn breakfast into a perfect loaf.

. . . .

1 **Make the porridge.** Bring the mixed porridge flakes, milk and 300ml of water to the boil in a small pan on a medium heat, stirring occasionally. As soon as the liquid starts to boil, remove the pan from the heat and pour the mixture through a sieve set over a bowl. Leave the porridge flakes in the sieve and the cooking liquid to cool to room temperature.

2 **Make the dough.** Tip the cooled porridge flakes into the bowl of a stand mixer, and add the flour, yeast, honey and salt. Add 250ml of the reserved porridge cooking liquid and stir to combine. Attach the bowl to the mixer fitted with the dough hook and mix on low–medium speed for 3–4 minutes, until nearly smooth.

3 Turn out the dough onto a clean work surface and knead it by hand for 3 minutes, until smooth and elastic – the dough will have texture from the oats. Do not be tempted to add more flour if the dough is sticky during kneading. Shape the dough into a ball, return it to the bowl, cover and leave it to rise for 4 hours, until doubled in size.

4 Tip the extra 50g of rolled flakes onto a plate and dust the inside of the lined proving basket or bowl with flour. Turn out the dough onto a floured work surface and knead it for 30 seconds to knock it back. Shape into a tight ball, lightly brush the top and sides with water and roll the dough ball in the oats to coat. Place in the floured proving basket or bowl, top-side down, cover with a damp tea towel or place in a proving bag and leave at room temperature for a further 2–3 hours, until nearly doubled in size.

5 Meanwhile, heat the oven to 220°C/200°C fan/Gas 7. Place the cloche or casserole in the oven to heat up at the same time.

6 **Make the loaf.** Place the baking paper disc on top of the basket, cover with a baking sheet and carefully turn the dough out of the basket onto the baking paper. Slide the loaf, still on the paper, into the hot cloche or casserole. Using sharp scissors, cut slashes into the top of the loaf, cover with the lid and bake for 40 minutes, until golden brown.

7 Reduce the oven to 200°C/180°C fan/Gas 6, remove the lid and bake for a further 10 minutes, until the bread is deep golden brown and crusty. Leave to cool on a wire rack before slicing.

Chocolate hazelnut brioche buns

Makes: 12
Hands on: 1 hour + rising
Bake: 25 mins

FOR THE DOUGH
3 tbsp dried milk powder
400g strong white bread flour
7g fast-action dried yeast
50g caster sugar
1 tsp salt
100ml whole milk,
    plus extra for glazing
50ml lukewarm water
2 eggs, lightly beaten
100g unsalted butter,
    cubed and softened
1 tsp vanilla paste

FOR THE FILLING AND TO DECORATE
100g blanched hazelnuts
4 tbsp chocolate hazelnut spread
2 tbsp pearl sugar

You will need
8–9cm non-stick crumpet
    or muffin rings x 12
large baking sheet, lined
    with baking paper
pizza wheel

This soft, buttery dough has toasted milk powder added to the mixture, which lends a lovely, nutty flavour. The swirls are most delicious eaten on the day, but, a day later, a quick reheat in the oven or microwave will revive them beautifully.

. . . .

1 **Make the dough.** Warm the milk powder in a non-stick frying pan on a low–medium heat, stirring continuously until the powder is toasted and golden. Tip it into a bowl and leave to cool.

2 Using a balloon whisk, mix the flour, milk powder, yeast, sugar and salt in the bowl of a stand mixer. Attach the bowl to the stand mixer, fit with the dough hook and make a well in the ingredients.

3 Heat the milk until lukewarm and pour it into the bowl. Add the water, eggs, butter and vanilla and mix on low until combined. Scrape down the inside of the bowl and knead for 7–8 minutes, until silky smooth and elastic, and it pulls away from the sides. Scrape down the bowl again, cover the dough and leave it to rise at room temperature for 1½–2 hours, until doubled in size.

4 Place the crumpet rings on the lined baking sheet.

5 Turn out the risen dough onto a floured work surface and roll it into a neat 40cm square, lightly flouring the work surface and rolling pin as needed. The dough will want to spring back, so roll it briefly, let it rest, then roll again until you reach the right size.

6 **Fill the dough.** Toast 50g of the hazelnuts in a frying pan for 5 minutes, turning occasionally, until golden, then finely chop. Roughly chop the remaining untoasted nuts and set aside.

7 Warm the chocolate spread in a microwave for 10 seconds to loosen, then spread it evenly over the top half of the dough square. Scatter the chopped, toasted hazelnuts over the chocolate spread. Fold the bottom half of the dough neatly over the nutty chocolate spread to make a 40 x 20cm rectangle.

8 Trim the dough to neaten the sides, then use the pizza wheel to cut it into 12 strips, each measuring 20 x 3cm. Take one strip of dough at a time and roll it away from you into a neat spiral. Tuck the end underneath and place it in the crumpet ring on the lined baking sheet. Repeat to make 12 buns. Cover with a tea towel and leave to rise at room temperature for 45 minutes, until doubled in size.

9 **Bake the swirls.** Heat the oven to 180°C/160°C fan/Gas 4. Brush the top of the buns with milk, scatter with the reserved chopped hazelnuts and the pearl sugar and bake for 25 minutes, until risen and golden. Leave the buns to cool for 2 minutes, then lift off the crumpet rings. Serve slightly warm.

French baguettes

Makes: 4
Hands on: 1 hour
   + rising and resting
Bake: 20 mins

500g strong white bread flour
2 tsp salt
8g fast-action dried yeast
350ml lukewarm water

You will need
thick tea towel or baker's couche
2 large baking trays, lined
   with baking paper
unlipped baking sheet,
   lightly floured
very sharp knife (not serrated),
   razor blade or lame

This recipe cherry picks from everything I've learned about breadmaking in the last few months. I love the contrast between the crisp crust and light middle in these baguettes – and the fact there is very little kneading involved!

· · · · · · · · · · ·

1 **Make the dough.** Combine the flour, salt and yeast in a large bowl. Mix in the lukewarm water using a clean hand until the mixture comes together into a ball.

2 Tip out the dough onto the work surface and knead it for 2 minutes, until smooth. Shape it into a ball, cupping your hands around the dough while you pull it towards you on the work surface to bring the sides under the base. Place the dough back in the bowl, round-side uppermost, cover and leave it to rise at room temperature for 45 minutes.

3 Turn the dough out of the bowl and knock it back into a flattish 20cm square. Taking each in turn, fold the corners into the middle of the square, turning the dough as you go. Repeat to make twelve folds in total, flip the dough over, shape it into a tight ball and return it to the bowl, seam-side down, then cover and leave it to rise for 45 minutes.

4 Repeat the folding process in Step 3, then return the dough to the bowl, cover and leave to rise for another 30 minutes.

5 **Shape the dough.** Turn the dough out of the bowl, knock it back, then shape it into a flattish square and divide it into four equal portions.

6 Very lightly flour the work surface and, working with one piece at a time, press each portion into a rectangle, about 24 x 12cm. Starting at the longer side furthest from you, roll the dough towards you into a tight spiral. After each two rolls fold in the top corners to keep the dough spiral tight and with tension – when the dough is fully rolled, the seam will be at the bottom.

7 Using the heel of your hand, gently press down on the seam to seal. Gently roll the dough on the work surface with your hands to taper the ends to resemble a traditional baguette shape.

8 Lay the cloth or couche on the work surface so that around 5cm at one end is vertical up against a wall, then dust it with flour. Lay the first baguette, seam-side down, against the wall end of the couche so that the bottom and one side of the baguette are in contact with the cloth. Create a 5cm-high pleat in the cloth next to the opposite side of the baguette – it should cradle the baguette, rather than cover it.

Continues overleaf

French baguettes
continued

9 Shape the remaining three portions of dough as in steps 6 to 8 and place them on the cloth with a pleat between each baguette. Cover the baguettes loosely and leave them to prove for 45 minutes to 1 hour, until the dough is puffy and has risen by about half.

10 **Bake the baguettes.** When you're ready to bake, heat the oven to 220°C/200°C fan/Gas 7 and put a roasting tin in the bottom of the oven.

11 Transfer the baguettes to the lined baking trays, using a flat (unlipped) lightly floured baking sheet to help move them to prevent the dough deflating. To do this, put the baking sheet next to the nearest baguette on the cloth and carefully flatten the pleat – the baguette will roll upside down onto the baking sheet. Gently roll the baguette onto the lined baking tray, seam-side down. Repeat, placing two baguettes on each baking tray with space between them to allow for rising during baking.

12 Lightly dust the top of each baguette with flour. Make four diagonal slashes along the top of each baguette using the sharp knife, razor blade or lame – these should be at a 70 degree angle and 1cm in from the sides.

13 Boil the kettle and fill the roasting tin with boiling water to create steam in the oven. Spray the inside of the oven and the top of each baguette with water and bake for 15–20 minutes, until the crust is crisp and deep golden. Leave the baguettes to cool on a wire rack before slicing.

Kale pesto & roasted red pepper babka

This savoury swirled loaf, made with buttery brioche-style dough and filled with nutty kale pesto and roasted peppers (a departure from the more traditional chocolate), is so much easier to achieve than it looks. And there's a bonus: you can use any leftover pesto to stir through soup or pasta.

. . . .

Makes: 1 loaf
Hands on: 45 mins + rising
Bake: 30 mins

FOR THE DOUGH
325g strong white bread flour
6g fast-action dried yeast
1 tsp salt, plus extra for
    seasoning the filling
pinch of caster sugar
125ml whole milk,
    plus 1 tbsp for glazing
2 eggs, lightly beaten
75g unsalted butter,
    cubed and softened
freshly ground black pepper

FOR THE PESTO
AND PEPPER FILLING
50g kale, stalks removed
    and leaves trimmed
15g flat-leaf parsley
1 tsp finely grated unwaxed
    lemon zest
25g blanched hazelnuts, toasted
2 garlic cloves, roughly chopped
pinch of dried chilli flakes
6 tbsp extra-virgin olive oil
60g parmesan, finely grated
2 jarred roasted red peppers,
    drained, cut into quarters,
    deseeded and patted dry

You will need
900g loaf tin, greased, then lined
    (base and sides) with baking paper
baking sheet, lined with baking paper

1 **Make the dough.** Mix the flour, yeast, salt, sugar and a good grinding of pepper in a stand mixer fitted with a dough hook.

2 Heat the milk in a small pan until lukewarm, then add it to the dry ingredients with the eggs. Mix on low–medium speed until just combined. Gradually add the butter and knead for 5 minutes, until the dough is silky smooth, elastic and cleanly leaves the sides of the bowl. Shape the dough into a ball, return it to the bowl, cover and leave to rise for 1 hour, until doubled in size.

3 **Prepare the filling.** While the dough is rising, blend the kale, parsley, lemon zest, hazelnuts, garlic and chilli flakes in a food processor until roughly chopped. Season with salt and pepper. Add the olive oil and 25g of the parmesan and blend again until just combined but still with a little texture. Cover and chill until ready to use.

4 **Fill the dough.** Tip out the dough onto a lightly floured work surface and knead it gently for 10 seconds. Roll the dough out to a neat 40 x 30cm rectangle, with one of the long sides nearest you. Spread 4–5 tablespoons of the pesto over the top (save any leftover pesto for another dish), reserve 1 tablespoon of the remaining parmesan and scatter the rest over the dough. Arrange the roasted peppers on top.

5 **Shape the dough.** As tightly as you can, roll up the dough, starting from the long edge and rolling it away from you. Place the roll, seam-side down, on the lined baking sheet and chill for 10 minutes to make shaping easier.

6 Return the dough to the work surface and, with a long, sharp knife, cut it lengthways in half. Turn each piece so that the cut side is facing upwards. Pinch the two pieces together at one end, then twist them together, keeping the cut sides facing upwards as you work down the length of the dough. Pinch the opposite end together, then carefully lift the twisted dough into the prepared tin. Loosely cover and prove for 1 hour, until risen by one-third.

7 **Bake the babka.** Heat the oven to 190°C/170°C fan/Gas 5. Gently brush the top of the loaf with milk and scatter over the rest of the parmesan. Bake for 30 minutes, until risen and golden. Leave the babka to cool in the tin for 10 minutes before lifting it out to cool on a wire rack. Serve warm or at room temperature.

Feta & za'atar flatbreads

Makes: 4
Hands on: 30 mins + resting
Cook: 15 mins

300g plain flour
2 tsp baking powder
1 tsp salt
½ tsp caster sugar
125g full-fat plain yogurt
100g feta, crumbled
3–4 tsp za'atar
2–3 tbsp extra-virgin olive oil

Thanks to the cooking method (superfast in a frying pan, then under a grill), these unleavened, yeast-free flatbreads are similar to a naan bread, but dispense with the need for a tandoor oven. The feta and za'atar flavours are out of this world. Serve them with dips or curry, or soups and salads.

. . . .

1 **Make the dough.** Sift the flour, baking powder, salt and sugar into a large bowl. Make a well in the middle of the dry ingredients, add the yogurt and 75ml of water and use your hand to combine. If needed, add up to 25ml of extra water to bring the mixture together into a smooth dough.

2 Turn out the dough onto the work surface and knead it for 3–4 minutes, until smooth (if the dough is sticky, lightly flour the work surface while kneading). Shape the dough into a smooth ball and return it to the bowl. Cover with a clean tea towel and leave to rest for 30 minutes.

3 Heat the grill to the highest setting and place a large, dry, ovenproof frying pan on a medium–high heat.

4 **Shape and cook the dough.** Divide the dough into four equal portions. Working one piece at a time, roll each into a thin flatbread, about 20cm in diameter. Place the flatbread in the hot frying pan and cook on one side for 1–2 minutes, until the underside is mottled with golden brown patches and the bread has started to puff up.

5 Working quickly, scatter over one-quarter of the feta and za'atar and drizzle with some olive oil. Place the frying pan under the hot grill and cook the top of the flatbread for 1 minute, until it is puffed up, bubbly and golden brown. Remove from the pan and keep warm.

6 To make the remaining flatbreads, roll out the next portion of dough. Wipe the pan clean and cook the flatbread as described in steps 4 and 5. Continue to make four flatbreads in total.

Cinnamon & raisin milk bread

Makes: 1 large loaf
Hands on: 1 hour + rising
Bake: 30 mins

FOR THE TANGZHONG
75ml whole milk
30g strong white bread flour

FOR THE DOUGH
350g strong white bread flour
100g strong wholemeal flour
20g dried milk powder
20g caster sugar
8g fast-action dried yeast
1 tbsp ground cinnamon
1 tsp salt
125ml whole milk,
    plus 1 tsp
3 eggs
100g unsalted butter,
    cubed and softened
100g raisins

You will need
900g loaf tin, greased, then
    lined (base and ends) with
    a strip of baking paper

Milk bread is one of my favourite breads. This malty loaf makes for great sandwiches and you can boujee it up with anything sweet or savoury. If you don't eat it all straightaway, it makes the best French toast when it goes stale.

· · · · · · · · · ·

1 **Make the tangzhong.** In a small pan, whisk the milk with 75ml of water and the flour until smooth. Set the pan on a low heat and cook, whisking continuously, for 30 seconds, until the mixture thickens to a thick, smooth paste. Spoon the tangzhong into a small bowl and leave to cool.

2 **Make the dough.** Mix both types of flour with the milk powder, sugar, yeast, cinnamon and salt in a stand mixer fitted with the dough hook, on medium speed, until combined.

3 Warm the 125ml of milk in a small pan and add it to the mixer bowl with two of the eggs, the butter and the cooled tangzhong, and mix on low speed to combine. Scrape down the inside of the bowl, increase the speed to medium and knead for 7 minutes, until the dough is smooth, glossy and elastic.

4 Tip out the dough onto the work surface and shape it into a ball. Return the dough to the bowl, cover, and leave it to rise at room temperature for 1–1½ hours, until doubled in size.

5 Lightly flour the work surface and tip out the dough again. Add the raisins, then knead gently to incorporate them evenly throughout the dough.

6 **Shape the dough.** Divide the dough into four equal portions. Roll one piece of dough into a 20cm square and fold in the left and right sides to meet in the middle, forming a rectangle measuring roughly 20 x 10cm. Starting from one of the shorter sides, roll up the dough into a neat spiral. Pinch the edge to seal and place, seam-side down at one end of the prepared loaf tin. Repeat with the remaining dough pieces, so you have four neat rolls in a row, running the length of the loaf tin. Loosely cover and leave to prove at room temperature for 1½ hours, until doubled in size and the dough has risen above the sides of the tin.

7 **Bake the loaf.** Heat the oven to 190°C/170°C fan/Gas 5. Beat the remaining egg with the 1 teaspoon of milk and lightly brush the glaze over the top of the loaf. Bake for 30 minutes, until risen and golden. Leave the loaf to cool in the tin for 10–15 minutes, then carefully lift it out onto a wire rack to cool completely before slicing.

Curry-spiced tear & share loaf

A stunning centrepiece, this feature bread is perfect to serve with curry or Indian chutneys and pickles. Creating the intertwined C-shapes isn't as fiddly as it looks, and the results are suitably impressive – set the loaf on the table, soak up the oohs and aahs, and tuck in.

. . . .

Makes: 1 large loaf
Hands on: 1 hour + rising
Bake: 25 mins

FOR THE DOUGH
350g strong white bread flour
100g plain flour
7g fast-action dried yeast
1 tsp caster sugar
1 tsp salt
½ tsp ground turmeric
300ml whole milk
25g unsalted butter, softened

FOR THE FILLING
2 onions, thinly sliced
75g unsalted butter
2 garlic cloves, crushed
1 green chilli, finely chopped
1 red chilli, finely chopped
50g unsweetened desiccated coconut
1 tbsp tomato purée
1 tsp cumin seeds
1 tsp dried fenugreek (methi) leaves
1 tsp garam or Punjab masala
    or curry powder
1 tsp pul biber or ½ tsp crushed
    dried chilli flakes
20 dried curry leaves
1 tsp nigella or black onion seeds
1 small bunch (30g) coriander,
    leaves chopped
juice of ½ lime
75g cheddar, coarsely grated
75g paneer, coarsely grated
salt and freshly ground black pepper

TO FINISH
1 egg beaten with 1 tbsp milk, to glaze
2 tsp chaat masala (optional)

You will need
large baking sheet, lined
    with baking paper

1 **Make the dough.** Mix both types of flour with the yeast, sugar, salt and turmeric in a stand mixer fitted with the dough hook until combined.

2 Heat the milk in a small pan until lukewarm. Add the warmed milk and the butter to the dry ingredients in the stand mixer and mix on low speed for 1 minute to combine, then increase the speed slightly and knead for 4–5 minutes, until the dough is smooth and elastic. Shape the dough into a ball, return it to the bowl, cover and leave it to rise for 1 hour, until doubled in size.

3 **Make the filling.** While the dough is rising, cook the onions with 25g of the butter in a frying pan on a low–medium heat for about 5–7 minutes, until soft but not coloured, stirring occasionally. Add the garlic and both types of chilli and cook for a further 1 minute. Add the coconut, tomato purée, spices, curry leaves and nigella or black onion seeds and cook for a further 1–2 minutes, stirring continuously, until aromatic. Remove from the heat, season with salt and pepper and add the coriander, lime juice and remaining butter. Mix to combine and leave to cool.

4 **Shape the dough.** Lightly flour the work surface and pat the dough into a rectangle. Slowly roll the dough into a neat 40 x 30cm rectangle with one of the long sides nearest you. Spread the cooled onion mixture evenly over the dough and scatter with the cheddar and paneer.

5 Starting with the bottom long edge, roll the dough into a neat tight log. Using a sharp knife, trim the ends. Without cutting all the way through the dough, cut the log into 25–30 slices, leaving the bottom 2cm attached. Cut the log in half and place one piece on the lined baking sheet in a semi-circle or 'C' shape, allowing the cut slices to fan open slightly. Arrange the second half of dough around the first in a backwards 'C' shape, leaving a small gap in the middle for the dough to rise. Cover loosely and leave for 1 hour, until puffy and increased in size by at least one-third.

6 **Bake the loaf.** Heat the oven to 190°C/170°C fan/Gas 5. Glaze the loaf with the egg wash and scatter with chaat masala, if using. Bake the loaf for 25 minutes, turning the tray halfway through baking so the bread cooks evenly, until risen and golden. Serve warm or at room temperature.

Dill-pickle brioche burger buns

People often think to upscale their burger patties with herbs, spices and other flavours, but what about the bread? These golden, tender burger buns have not only pickles baked into the dough, but also crispy onions, garlic and dill, making them as much a part of the experience as the patty itself.

Makes: 15
Hands on: 30 mins + rising
Bake: 20 mins

FOR THE TANGZHONG
75ml whole milk
25g strong white bread flour

FOR THE DOUGH
500g strong white bread flour
7g fast-action dried yeast
1 tbsp caster sugar
2 tsp salt
2 tsp dried dill
1 tsp garlic granules
175ml whole milk
1 egg and 1 yolk, lightly beaten
3 tbsp burger pickle juice
75g unsalted butter,
    cubed and softened
sunflower oil, for oiling
3 tbsp crispy fried onions
100g gherkin burger pickle,
    finely chopped

FOR THE TOPPING
1 egg, beaten
1 tbsp sesame seeds

You will need
2 baking sheets, lined
    with baking paper
2 proving bags (optional)

1 **Make the tangzhong.** In a small pan, whisk the milk with 50ml of water and the flour until smooth. Set the pan on a low heat and cook, whisking continuously, for 30 seconds, until the mixture thickens to a smooth, thick paste. Spoon the tangzhong into a small bowl and leave to cool.

2 **Make the dough.** Mix the flour, yeast, sugar, salt, dill and garlic granules in a stand mixer fitted with the dough hook to combine.

3 Heat the milk in a small pan until lukewarm, then add it to the stand mixer with the beaten egg and yolk, burger pickle juice, cooled tangzhong and butter. Mix on low to combine, then increase the speed to medium and knead for 7 minutes, until the dough is smooth, glossy and elastic.

4 Tip out the dough onto a lightly floured work surface and shape it into a ball. Lightly oil the bowl, return the dough to it, and cover and leave the dough to rise at room temperature for 1½ hours, until doubled in size.

5 **Flavour the dough.** When the dough has risen, return the bowl to the stand mixer. Add the fried onions and chopped burger pickle and mix on low speed until the onion and gherkin are evenly distributed throughout the dough.

6 **Make the buns.** Tip out the dough onto a lightly floured work surface, then divide it into 15 portions, about 75g each. Shape each portion into a round bun with the seal on the underside.

7 Arrange the buns on the lined baking sheets, allowing space between each one. Place each sheet in a proving bag or cover loosely with a tea towel and leave the buns to prove at room temperature for 45–60 minutes, until risen, puffy and nearly doubled in size.

8 **Bake the buns.** Heat the oven to 190°C/170°C fan/Gas 5. Lightly brush the top of each bun with beaten egg and scatter over the sesame seeds. Bake for 20 minutes, until risen and golden, then transfer to a wire rack to cool. Serve the buns split in half and toasted, then filled with your choice of burger and yummy fillings.

Pear, taleggio & walnut sourdough focaccia

Makes: 1 large loaf
Hands on: 1 hour + resting
  and overnight proving
Bake: 30 mins

450ml lukewarm water
150g active sourdough starter
600g strong white bread flour
12g sea-salt flakes, finely crushed,
  plus extra to decorate
75ml extra-virgin olive oil
75g shelled walnuts
2 rosemary sprigs
150g taleggio or brie
1 ripe pear
1–2 tbsp runny honey (optional)

You will need
33 x 23cm baking tin, about 6cm
  deep, lined (base and sides)
  with baking paper
dough scraper

This treat of a slow-proved focaccia is delicious just as it is, warm from the oven. Feel free to swap in your own favourite nuts or soft cheese, as you prefer. You'll need an active sourdough starter (see page 227) before you begin.

· · · · · · · · · · · ·

1 **Make the dough.** Whisk the water and sourdough starter in a large bowl using a balloon whisk until combined. Using a damp hand or silicone spatula, mix in the flour until almost combined – it will be slightly lumpy at this point. Cover and set aside for 30 minutes to allow the flour to hydrate.

2 Add the salt and a further 25ml of water and, using a damp hand, knead the dough in the bowl until smooth. Scrape down the inside of the bowl using a dough scraper or silicone spatula, then cover and rest the dough for another 30 minutes.

3 **Stretch and fold the dough.** With the dough still in the bowl, and using a wet hand, pick the top edge of the dough up, stretch it out slightly, then fold it over the dough to meet the bottom edge. Turn the bowl 90 degrees clockwise and repeat this stretching and folding a further three times, turning the bowl between each fold. Cover and leave the dough to rest for 30 minutes.

4 Repeat this sequence of stretching and folding a further three times, each set 30 minutes apart, completing four sets of folds over a 2-hour period. Cover the bowl and leave the dough to ferment at room temperature for 45 minutes. Next, place the dough in the fridge to slow prove for 10 hours or overnight, until almost doubled in size.

5 **Shape the dough.** Pour 3–4 tablespoons of the olive oil into the lined baking tin to coat the base and sides. Using a dough scraper, scoop the dough into the tin, then press it out with damp hands until level and it almost reaches the corners. Cover and leave for 1–3 hours (depending on the temperature of your room), until risen to fill the tin and the surface looks bubbly.

6 Meanwhile, roughly chop the walnuts and rosemary leaves, dice the cheese and quarter, core and slice the pear. Heat the oven to 220°C/200°C fan/Gas 7.

7 **Bake the focaccia.** Using oiled fingers, gently press the dough to make dimples over the top, then scatter with the walnuts, rosemary, cheese and pear. Drizzle with the remaining oil, scatter with sea-salt flakes and bake for 30 minutes, until golden brown and well risen.

8 Remove the focaccia from the tin and leave it to cool on a wire rack for 30 minutes, then drizzle it with honey, if using, and cut it into slices or squares to serve.

4
Pastry

Curried vegetable pie

Filled with aromatic curried vegetables, pulses and paneer, this vegetable pie is topped with an intricate lattice. It needs some concentration, but the stunning results are worth the effort. Serve the pie warm with chutneys, pickles and raita.

. . . .

Serves: 6
Hands on: 2 hours + chilling
Bake: 55 mins

FOR THE FILLING
500g peeled and diced
    butternut squash
275g waxy potatoes, such as
    Charlotte, peeled and diced
3 tbsp olive oil
2 onions, sliced
2 large garlic cloves, crushed
7.5cm piece of fresh ginger, grated
1 large green chilli, finely chopped
1 tsp cumin seeds
1 tsp hot chilli powder
½ tsp ground turmeric
½ tsp ground coriander
½ tsp ground cardamom
1 tbsp dried curry leaves
400g can of chopped tomatoes
400ml vegetable stock or water
2 tbsp tamarind paste
125g cooked brown lentils
125g canned drained chickpeas
150g paneer cheese, diced
100g baby leaf spinach
2 tbsp chopped coriander
salt and freshly ground black pepper

FOR THE PASTRY
450g plain flour
1 tsp ground turmeric
1 tsp curry powder
300g unsalted butter,
    chilled and cubed
6–7 tbsp ice-cold water
2 tsp cider or white wine vinegar
1 egg beaten with 1 tbsp whole
    milk, to glaze
1 tbsp nigella or black onion seeds

You will need
large baking tray
round pie tin (about 27cm diameter
    at the top and 20cm at the base)
pizza wheel

1 **Make the filling.** Heat the oven to 190°C/170°C fan/Gas 5. Tip the squash and potatoes into the baking tray, drizzle over half of the oil and season with salt and pepper. Mix to coat the vegetables in the oil and roast for 30 minutes, turning halfway through, until the vegetables are tender and starting to turn golden at the edges.

2 Meanwhile, heat the remaining oil in a large pan on a low–medium heat. Add the onions and cook, stirring often, for about 5–7 minutes, until soft but not coloured. Add the garlic, ginger and chilli and cook for 1 minute. Stir in the dried spices and curry leaves and cook for 1 minute more.

3 Add the chopped tomatoes, vegetable stock or water and tamarind paste and slowly bring the liquid to the boil. Reduce the heat to low and simmer for 20 minutes, stirring often. Add the roasted squash and potatoes to the pan, along with the lentils, chickpeas and paneer, stir and cook for a further 10 minutes.

4 Taste the filling mixture and season with salt and pepper, as necessary. Add the spinach and cook for 1 minute, until wilted. Spoon the filling into a bowl, leave to cool, then mix in the coriander, and chill until you're ready to assemble the pie.

5 **Prepare the pastry.** While the filling is cooling, tip the flour and spices into a large bowl and season with salt and pepper. Using your fingertips, rub in the butter until the mixture resembles breadcrumbs, with small flecks of butter remaining. Stir in the iced water and vinegar using a table knife and when the pastry starts to clump together, use your hands to gather the mixture into a ball. Flatten the pastry into a disc, then wrap it and chill it for 1 hour, until firm.

6 **Assemble the pie.** Lightly dust the work surface with flour and cut the pastry in half. Roll one half of the pastry into a neat round, large enough to line the base and sides of the pie tin with a 5cm excess all round. Using the rolling pin, lift the pastry into the tin, pressing it into the base and up the sides and allowing the excess to hang over the edge. Spoon the cold filling into the pie and flatten the top. (Freeze any excess pie filling to use another time.)

Continues overleaf

Curried
vegetable
pie
continued

7 **Start the herringbone lattice pastry top.** Roll the remaining pastry into a neat 45 x 30cm rectangle and, using the pizza wheel, cut it into twenty 2 x 30cm strips. Lay half of the pastry strips vertically across the top of the pie, placing them side-by-side to cover the filling.

8 To start the lattice: lift the first vertical pastry strip on the left-hand side of the pie and fold it in half over itself. Skip the next three strips of pastry, then fold the next three strips of pastry in half, skip the next three strips and continue until you reach the right-hand edge of the pie. There should be a straight line of folded pastry strips across the centre of the pie.

9 Start the horizontal rows, working downwards from the middle. Place one strip of pastry horizontally across the middle of the pie, so it is snug against the folded-over strips, then unfold the vertical strips back down to cover.

10 For row two: start at the left-hand side, fold the first two strips up and over, skip three, then fold the following three strips over and continue until you reach the right-hand side. Place the second horizontal strip across the vertical strips, up against the folds. Fold the verticals back down to cover.

11 For row three: start at the left again, fold the first three vertical strips up and over the horizontal strips, skip three, then fold three as before. Position another horizontal against the folds and reposition the vertical strips over it.

12 For row four: skip the first left-hand vertical strip, fold the next three and repeat. Position another horizontal against the folds and reposition the vertical strips over it.

13 For row five: skip the first two left-hand strips, fold the next three, skip three and repeat until you reach the right-hand side. Position another horizontal strip and fold back the vertical strips. By now you should have covered the bottom half of the pie with a lattice with 10 vertical and 5 horizontal strips of pastry.

14 **Lattice the other half of the pie.** Start at the left-hand side, skip the first three strips, then fold the next three back over onto the lattice, skip three, then fold the next three as before. Position a horizontal strip and unfold the verticals over it.

15 For row two: skip the first two verticals, fold the next three and repeat in threes. Lay over a horizontal and repeat.

16 For row three: skip the first vertical strip, fold the next three verticals and repeat in threes, position a horizontal strip and reset the verticals.

17 For row four: fold back the first three strips, skip three, fold three and continue to the opposite side. Position the horizontal and unfold the verticals.

18 For row five: repeat the next row, folding back the first two strips, skipping three, folding three. By this point, you should have covered the top of the pie, but if you need to add another row, fold back the first strip, skip three and fold three.

19 Once the pie is covered in the herringbone pastry lattice, pat yourself on the back! Using a sharp knife, trim the excess pastry around the edge with a sharp knife. Lightly brush the ends of the lattice strips with water, then press the edges together to seal. Brush the pie all over with the egg glaze, scatter with the nigella or black onion seeds and chill for 30 minutes while you heat the oven to 190°C/170°C fan/Gas 5. Place a baking sheet in the oven to heat at the same time.

20 **Bake the pie.** Carefully place the pie on the hot baking sheet and bake for 30 minutes, then reduce the oven to 180°C/160°C fan/Gas 4. Bake for another 20–25 minutes, until the pastry is crisp and golden, and the filling bubbling hot. Serve hot or warm.

Mini sausage & egg pies

These are definitely not your average pork pies! Filled with spicy, herby sausagemeat and a quail's egg, these little pastry parcels are ideal for picnics and summer parties.

. . . .

Makes: 12
Hands on: 40 mins + chilling
Bake: 30 mins

FOR THE PASTRY
350g plain flour
½ tsp English mustard powder
½ tsp cayenne
200g unsalted butter,
    cubed and chilled
4 tbsp ice-cold water
1 tsp cider or white wine vinegar
1 egg yolk
1 egg beaten with 1 tbsp
    whole milk, to glaze
salt and freshly ground
    black pepper

FOR THE FILLING
12 quail's eggs, at room temperature
250g good-quality sausagemeat
250g cooking chorizo sausagemeat
6 spring onions, finely chopped
1 garlic clove, crushed
2 tsp Dijon mustard
2 tbsp chopped flat-leaf parsley
2 tsp chopped thyme leaves

You will need
11cm plain round cutter
8cm plain round cutter
12-hole muffin tin,
    preferably non-stick

1 **Make the pastry.** Tip the flour, mustard powder and cayenne into a large bowl and season with salt and pepper. Stir until combined, then cut the butter into the flour with a table knife until the pieces are half their original size. Using your fingertips, rub in the butter until the mixture resembles breadcrumbs, with small flecks of butter remaining. Stir in the ice-cold water, vinegar and egg yolk with the table knife and, when the pastry starts to clump together, use your hands to gather the mixture into a ball. Flatten the pastry into a disc, wrap it and chill it for 1 hour, until firm.

2 **Make the filling.** While the pastry is chilling, cook the quail's eggs in a small pan of boiling salted water for 2 minutes, then drain and refresh them under cold running water until they are completely cold. Carefully peel the eggs, then cover and chill them until needed.

3 Tip both types of sausagemeat into a large bowl. Add the spring onions, garlic, Dijon mustard and herbs. Season well and mix to combine.

4 Divide the pastry into two unequal pieces, of one-third and two-thirds. Lightly flour the work surface and roll out the larger piece of pastry until it is 2mm thick. Using the larger cutter, stamp out pastry discs, re-rolling when needed, until you have 12 discs in total. Line the base and sides of each hole in the muffin tin with the cut-out pastry discs. Roll out the second piece of pastry and stamp out twelve 8cm discs to make the pie lids.

5 **Assemble the pies.** Divide the sausagemeat filling in half and portion it equally between the pastry cases. Nestle an egg into each one, then gently cover the eggs with the remaining sausagemeat, mounding it slightly in the middle of each pie

6 Brush the edges of each pastry lid with water and lay these on top of the pies, pressing the edges to seal. Make a small hole in the top of each pie with a skewer and chill the pies for 20 minutes. Meanwhile, heat the oven to 190°C/170°C fan/Gas 5.

7 **Bake the pies.** Brush the tops of the pies with the egg wash and bake them for 30 minutes, until the pastry is crisp and golden. Leave to cool slightly in the tin before removing and serving warm or cold.

Paul's dauphinoise potato & caramelised onion pithivier

This iteration of a 17th-century French pithivier (from the town of the same name) comprises dauphinoise encased in two discs of cheat's rough puff. The creamy cooking liquid is reinvented as a rich roquefort sauce.

Serves: 8–10
Hands on: 45 mins
   + cooling and chilling
Bake: 40 mins

FOR THE FILLING
750g Charlotte potatoes
300ml double cream
300ml whole milk
2 garlic cloves, finely chopped
1 tbsp olive oil
large knob of unsalted butter
2 onions, finely sliced
freshly grated nutmeg
crushed sea salt and freshly
   ground black pepper

**FOR THE CHEAT'S ROUGH
PUFF PASTRY**
400g plain flour
pinch of salt
65g unsalted butter,
   cubed and chilled
120–150ml ice-cold water
160g frozen unsalted
   butter, grated
1 egg, beaten to glaze

FOR THE SAUCE
10g unsalted butter
10g plain flour
75g roquefort
2 tbsp chopped tarragon leaves

You will need
baking sheet, lined
   with baking paper

1 **Make the filling.** Slice the potatoes very thinly either by hand or using a mandoline. Heat the cream, milk and garlic in a large pan. Add the potatoes, bring to the boil, then reduce the heat and simmer gently for 10–15 minutes, until the potatoes are tender but not soft. Drain the potatoes in a sieve, reserving the milky liquid. Spread the potatoes out on a large tray to cool, then chill until needed.

2 Heat the oil and butter in a large frying pan. Add the onions and cook on a low heat for 20 minutes, until soft, translucent and lightly caramelised. Remove from the heat and leave to cool, then chill until needed.

3 **Make the cheat's rough puff.** While the filling is chilling, mix the flour and salt together in a large bowl. Rub in the chilled butter using your fingertips until the mixture resembles breadcrumbs. Gradually add enough of the ice-cold water to form a ball of dough.

4 Lightly flour the work surface and roll the dough out to a 45 x 15cm rectangle.

5 Scatter half of the frozen grated butter over the bottom two-thirds of the dough. Fold down the top third and fold up the bottom third as if folding a letter.

6 Turn the folded dough 90 degrees and roll it out again into a 45 x 15cm rectangle. Repeat the process, adding the remaining frozen butter and fold as before. Wrap the dough and leave it to chill in the fridge for 30 minutes.

7 Repeat the rolling and folding process one more time, this time without the butter. Wrap the dough and leave it to chill in the fridge for 30 minutes.

8 **Assemble the pithivier.** Lightly flour the work surface and roll out just under half (two-fifths) of the pastry until about 3mm thick, then cut out a 26cm-diameter disc. Place the disc on the lined baking sheet and cover it with a sheet of baking paper. Roll out the remaining pastry and cut a second disc, about 28cm in diameter. Set the larger disc aside.

9 Layer the cold potatoes and onions on top of the smaller pastry disc, seasoning them between each layer with salt

Continues overleaf

Paul's dauphinoise potato & caramelised onion pithivier
continued

and pepper and a sprinkling of nutmeg. Aim to create a slightly domed shape and leave a 2cm border around the edge. Brush the pastry border with beaten egg, then gently lay the larger pastry disc over the filling. Press the edges firmly together to seal, then brush the top with beaten egg.

10 Scallop the base by using your index finger to push down on the edge of the pastry and the finger and thumb of your other hand to pinch the pastry either side.

11 Holding a small knife blade at right angles to the side of the pastry, 'knock up' the edges by making small indentations around the base. Brush the top of the pastry with more beaten egg to glaze, then chill the pithivier for 30 minutes.

12 Brush the top again with the beaten egg and make a small hole in the centre of the domed top. Using the tip of a knife, score curved lines over the top, running downwards from the hole in the middle to the base, and taking care not to cut all the way through the pastry. Brush the top with beaten egg, then chill the pithivier for a further 30 minutes.

13 Meanwhile, heat the oven to 200°C/180°C fan/Gas 6.

14 Bake the pithivier for 35–40 minutes, until the pastry is golden and crisp.

15 **Make the sauce.** While the pithivier is baking, melt the butter in a small pan on a medium heat. Add the flour and stir with a wooden spoon to a paste. Stir the paste over a low heat for 2–3 minutes to cook out the flour flavour, then gradually add the reserved milky liquid (from Step 1), stirring continuously to a smooth sauce. Add the roquefort and tarragon and season to taste with pepper (it shouldn't need salt).

16 Remove the baked pithivier from the oven and leave it to cool slightly before serving with the sauce for pouring over.

Med-veg tarte tatin

It may be French and sound trés fancy, but this tarte tatin is as easy as it is delish. I love it because the sweet glaze with the savoury Mediterranean veg and buttery pastry makes for my favourite kind of flavour explosion.

Serves: 6–8
Hands on: 1 hour + chilling
Bake: 50 mins

FOR THE ROUGH PUFF PASTRY
225g plain flour
¼ tsp salt
45g unsalted butter,
    cubed and chilled
6 tbsp ice-cold water
90g frozen unsalted
    butter, grated

FOR THE GLAZE
3 tbsp balsamic vinegar
2 tbsp runny honey
juice of 1 orange
1 tsp caster sugar

FOR THE TOPPING
2 aubergines, trimmed and
    cut into 1.5cm-thick rounds
1 courgette, trimmed and
    cut into 1.5cm-thick rounds
1 red onion, cut into 6 wedges
    lengthways through the
    root and stem
about 3 tbsp olive oil
6 chestnut mushrooms, sliced
2 large tomatoes, thickly sliced
salt and freshly ground
    black pepper
small handful of oregano
    or basil leaves, to serve

You will need
2 baking sheets, lined
    with baking paper
25cm ovenproof frying pan

1 **Make the rough puff pastry.** Mix the flour and salt together in a bowl. Rub in the chilled butter using your fingertips until the mixture resembles breadcrumbs. Gradually, mix in the ice-cold water with a table knife. When the pastry starts to clump together, gather it into a ball (you may not need all the water).

2 On a lightly floured work surface, roll out the dough into a rectangle, about 40 x 15cm. Scatter half of the frozen grated butter over the bottom two-thirds of the dough. Fold down the top third and fold up the bottom third, as if folding a letter.

3 Turn the folded dough by 90 degrees and roll it out again into a 40 x 15cm rectangle. Repeat the process, adding the remaining frozen butter and folding as before. Wrap the dough and leave it to rest in the fridge for 30 minutes.

4 Repeat the rolling and folding process once more, but without the butter, and chill for a final 30 minutes to rest.

5 **Make the glaze.** While the pastry is chilling, combine the ingredients for the glaze in a small pan. Bring the liquid to the boil over a low–medium heat and cook until the glaze thickens and reduces by half. Leave to cool.

6 **Make the topping.** Heat the oven to 200°C/180°C fan/Gas 6. Arrange the aubergines, courgette and onion in a single layer on the lined baking trays, drizzle with 2 tablespoons of the olive oil and roast for 15 minutes, until softened and starting to brown. Add the mushrooms to the tray, drizzle with the remaining oil and roast for a further 5 minutes. Leave the vegetables to cool.

7 **Assemble the tatin.** Drizzle half of the glaze over the base of the frying pan and arrange the cooled roasted vegetables and raw tomatoes on top. Season well with salt and pepper and drizzle with the remaining glaze.

8 Lightly flour the work surface and roll out the pastry into a 38cm disc, about 3mm thick. Lay the pastry over the vegetables and tuck the edges down the inside of the pan. Make three small holes in the top of the pastry to allow steam to escape and bake the tatin for 25–30 minutes, until the pastry is risen, crisp and golden. Leave the tatin to rest for 2 minutes.

9 Place a board or serving plate on top of the pan and carefully flip the pan to turn out the tart. Scatter with the herbs to serve.

Cheesy leek pastries

Makes: 12
Hands on: 1½ hours + overnight
    resting, chilling and proving
Bake: 25 mins

FOR THE DOUGH
500g strong white bread flour
25g caster sugar
7g fast-action dried yeast
2 tsp salt
150ml whole milk
275g unsalted butter

FOR THE FILLING
25g unsalted butter
1 tbsp olive oil
3 leeks, cut into 1cm-thick slices
3 fat garlic cloves, crushed
3 rosemary sprigs, leaves picked
1 bushy thyme sprig, leaves picked
100g full-fat cream cheese
100g gruyère, finely grated
salt and freshly ground black pepper

TO FINISH
1 egg, beaten with 1 tbsp whole
    milk, to glaze
2 rosemary sprigs, leaves picked
2 tsp sea-salt flakes

You will need
pizza wheel
2 baking sheets, lined
    with baking paper

Making croissant dough is a labour of love, patience and precision – and is enormously satisfying. These butter pastries are filled with slow-cooked leeks and nutty gruyère cheese and make a wonderful weekend brunch, or a lunch or teatime treat.

. . . .

1 **Make the dough.** Mix the flour, sugar, yeast and salt in a stand mixer fitted with a dough hook. Heat the milk with 160ml of water in a small pan until lukewarm. Add 25g of the butter (chill the rest) and leave it for 30 seconds, until melted slightly. Pour the warm milk mixture into the bowl and mix on low–medium speed to combine. Scrape down the inside of the bowl and continue to mix for 3 minutes, until the ingredients are combined and the dough is nearly smooth. Turn the dough out of the bowl, shape it into a 20cm square and place it in a lightly oiled tray or plastic box. Cover and chill for at least 4 hours, or overnight.

2 **Make the filling.** While the dough is chilling, melt the 25g of butter with the olive oil in a large frying pan on a low–medium heat. Add the leeks and cook for 20–30 minutes, stirring often, until soft but not coloured. Add the garlic, rosemary and thyme and cook for a further 1 minute. Season well and leave to cool, then chill until you're ready to assemble the pastries.

3 **Continue with the dough.** Divide the remaining chilled butter into 2 x 125g blocks. Cut one block into 1cm-thick slices, then lay the slices side-by-side on a sheet of baking paper and cover with more paper. Using a rolling pin, press and roll the butter into a neat 18 x 12cm rectangle. Wrap and chill the rolled-out butter, while you repeat this with the second block. Chill for 30 minutes.

4 Divide the dough into two equal portions, then wrap and return one half to the fridge. On a lightly floured work surface, roll out one piece of the dough into a neat rectangle, about 30 x 20cm. With one of the long sides nearest you, place one chilled butter portion in the middle of the dough in a portrait rotation (a short side closest to you). Fold the left-hand side of the dough over into the middle of the butter and the right-hand side over to meet it, then press the join together to seal in the butter.

5 Flour the work surface again as needed. Starting from the middle, tap the dough with the rolling pin to flatten it, then gently roll it into a neat rectangle, about 45 x 15cm, keeping the edges neat and straight.

6 Fold down the top quarter of the dough, then fold the bottom edge up to it. Gently press the ends together and brush off any

Continues overleaf

Cheesy leek pastries
continued

excess flour. Fold the dough in half so that you now have a parcel that is four layers thick. Turn the dough 90° clockwise so that the open side is on the right. Wrap and chill it for 30–45 minutes, until the butter firms up. Meanwhile, repeat this rolling and folding with the other piece of dough and butter, then chill.

7 Lightly flour the work surface and place the first piece of dough with the open side on the right. Roll it out into a neat rectangle three times as long as it is wide (about 45 x 15cm). Fold the top of the dough down to cover two-thirds of the rectangle and the bottom third up to cover. Wrap and chill, then repeat with the second piece of dough. Chill the dough for at least 1 hour, or until needed.

8 **Make the pastries.** Lightly flour the work surface, roll one piece of the dough into a neat rectangle of about 40 x 30cm, with a short side nearest you. Spread half of the cream cheese over the bottom half of the dough and scatter with half of the cooked leeks and half of the gruyère. Fold the top of the dough over to cover the fillings and press the edges together to seal. Using a pizza wheel or sharp knife, cut the dough vertically into six 5cm-wide strips. Cut each strip vertically in half again, leaving 1–2cm uncut at the top of each strip. Working from the top of one strip of dough at a time, twist the cut strips together in a loose rope, then pinch the ends together to seal. Repeat with the second piece of dough to make 12 pastries in total. Place these on the lined baking sheets, cover them loosely and leave them at room temperature for 45 minutes to 1 hour, until the dough puffs up by about one-third.

9 Heat the oven to 190°C/170°C fan/Gas 5. Brush the pastries with the egg wash, scatter with the rosemary and sea salt and bake for 20–25 minutes, until crisp and golden. Serve warm or at room temperature.

Caramel latte cream puffs

Makes: 12–15
Hands on: 2½ hours + chilling
Bake: 25 mins

FOR THE CARAMEL
150g caster sugar
100ml double cream
pinch of salt
25g unsalted butter

FOR THE COFFEE CRÈME
400ml whole milk
3 cardamom pods, crushed
1 tsp vanilla paste
50g caster sugar
4 egg yolks
3 tbsp cornflour
25g unsalted butter
2 tsp instant espresso powder
    dissolved in 1 tsp boiling water
250g mascarpone

FOR THE CRAQUELIN TOPPING
40g unsalted butter, softened
50g light brown soft sugar
50g plain flour
25g blanched hazelnuts,
    very finely chopped
pinch of salt
2 tbsp icing sugar, sifted,
    plus extra for serving

FOR THE CHOUX PASTRY BUNS
100ml whole milk
75g unsalted butter,
    cubed and softened
1 tsp caster sugar
pinch of salt
125g plain flour, sifted
4 eggs, lightly beaten

Continues overleaf

Inspired by simple choux buns, these cream puffs are like profiteroles that have been given the pamper treatment – and the results are good enough to grace any Parisian patisserie window. There are a number of stages in the bake, but you can prepare each part ahead of time, so that all you have to do is to fill the puffs before serving.

. . . .

1 **Make the caramel.** Warm the sugar with 1 tablespoon of water in a pan on a low–medium heat, without stirring, until the sugar dissolves. Brush the sides of the pan with hot water if any crystals form. Continue to cook until you have an amber-coloured caramel, swirling the pan occasionally to ensure the sugar syrup cooks evenly. Working quickly, slide the pan off the heat and carefully stir the cream, salt and butter into the caramel until smooth. Return the pan to a low heat to melt any hardened caramel, then pour it into a bowl and leave it to cool.

2 **Make the coffee crème.** Meanwhile, heat the milk with the cardamom pods and vanilla until just boiling. Remove the pan from the heat and leave the milk to infuse for 30 minutes.

3 Reheat the milk mixture to just boiling. In a bowl, whisk the sugar, egg yolks and cornflour until smooth and creamy. Whisking continuously, pour half of the hot milk into the bowl until smooth. Return the mixture to the pan and whisk over a low heat until the crème starts to bubble and thicken. Continue to cook, stirring for 1 minute to cook out the cornflour. Remove from the heat, mix in the butter, coffee and caramel sauce, then pass it all through a fine-mesh sieve into a clean bowl. Cover the surface with a disc of baking paper to prevent a skin forming, leave to cool, then chill the coffee crème for at least 4 hours.

4 **Make the craquelin topping.** In a small bowl, beat the butter with the brown sugar until creamy. Mix in the flour, hazelnuts and salt, then lightly knead the dough until it's smooth. Flatten it into a disc, then roll it between two sheets of baking paper until 1–2mm thick. Chill the topping for 30 minutes.

5 Heat the oven to 190°C/170°C fan/Gas 5.

6 **Make the choux pastry.** Heat the milk, butter, sugar and salt with 100ml of water in a pan on a medium heat. Stir to melt the butter, then bring the mixture to a rolling boil. Immediately slide the pan off the heat and quickly beat in the flour with a wooden spoon, mixing until the batter is smooth. Return the pan to a low heat and cook, stirring continuously for 20–30 seconds, until the mixture is glossy and cleanly leaves the sides of the pan.

Continues overleaf

Caramel latte cream puffs
continued

FOR THE GANACHE
100g 70% dark chocolate,
    finely chopped
125ml double cream
10g unsalted butter
2 tsp caster sugar

FOR THE CARAMELISED HAZELNUTS
50g caster sugar
15 blanched hazelnuts

You will need
2 large piping bags, each fitted
    with a large open star nozzle
2 baking sheets, lined
    with baking paper
4.5cm plain cutter
small piping bag fitted with
    a medium star nozzle

7 Tip the choux mixture into a large bowl and leave it to cool for 5 minutes. Gradually add the eggs, mixing well between each addition, until the batter is silky smooth and reluctantly drops off a spoon – you may not need to add the last 2–3 teaspoons of egg. Scoop the mixture into a piping bag fitted with the large open star nozzle and pipe 12–15 small egg-sized mounds onto the lined baking sheets.

8 Using the plain cutter, stamp out 12–15 discs from the chilled craquelin topping and place one disc on top of each choux pastry bun. Dust the buns with the 2 tablespoons of icing sugar and bake them for 25 minutes, until risen, golden and crisp. Leave to cool.

9 **Make the ganache.** While the choux are cooling, tip the chocolate into a heatproof bowl. Heat the cream, butter and sugar in a small pan until just boiling, then pour the mixture over the chocolate and leave it to melt for 5 minutes. Stir the ganache until it's smooth, then set it aside until thick enough to pipe. Spoon the ganache into the small piping bag with the medium star nozzle.

10 Using a serrated knife, cut the top off each choux bun and pipe 1 teaspoon of the ganache into the bottom of each. To finish the filling, whisk the mascarpone until smooth and fold it into the chilled coffee crème. Spoon the crème into the other large piping bag fitted with the large open star nozzle and pipe the crème into each bun to fill. Cover each one with a lid and pipe the remaining ganache on top.

11 **Make the caramelised hazelnuts.** Melt the sugar with 1 tablespoon of water in a small frying pan on a low heat. Bring to the boil and cook, without stirring, until you have an amber caramel. Working quickly, add the hazelnuts, turning them to coat, then, using a fork, quickly remove them to a re-lined baking sheet. Leave the caramelised hazelnuts to cool.

12 To finish, decorate each choux bun with a caramelised hazelnut, dust the buns with icing sugar and serve.

Stuffed crust quiche

Serves: 6–8
Hands on: 1½ hours + chilling
Bake: 45 mins

FOR THE PASTRY
275g plain flour
150g unsalted butter, cubed and chilled
4–5 tbsp ice-cold water
1 tsp cider vinegar
200g spreadable soft goat's cheese
½ tsp garlic granules
1 tsp dried parsley
2 tbsp whole milk, for brushing
salt and freshly ground black pepper

FOR THE FILLING
2 red peppers, quartered, deseeded and cut into bite-sized pieces
1 tbsp olive oil
bunch of spring onions (about 6–8), trimmed
2 eggs
2 egg yolks
200ml double cream
8 Peppadew peppers from a jar, drained, patted dry and halved
1 courgette, cut into long ribbons
50g gruyère, grated
1 red chilli, deseeded and thinly sliced

You will need
piping bag fitted with a medium plain nozzle
large baking sheet, lined with baking paper
25cm round bowl (to use as a template)
baking beans

You've heard of stuffed-crust pizza – well here is a cheesy stuffed-crust quiche. And it even requires no tin.

. . . .

1 **Make the pastry case.** Tip the flour into a large bowl and season with salt and pepper. Cut the butter into the flour with a table knife, then rub it in with your fingertips until the mixture resembles breadcrumbs. Stir in the water and vinegar and use your hands to gather the mixture into a ball. Flatten the pastry into a disc, wrap and chill for 1 hour, until firm.

2 Meanwhile, beat the goat's cheese with the garlic granules and parsley until smooth, then spoon into the piping bag.

3 Lightly flour the work surface and roll out the pastry into a neat 40cm disc, about 2–3mm thick. Transfer the pastry to the lined baking sheet. Press the 25cm-diameter bowl into the dough to make a circular indent, leaving an even border around the edge. Pipe a ring of the goat's cheese mixture on top of the indent.

4 Using a sharp knife, trim the pastry disc slightly to neaten the edge. Imagine the pastry as a clock face, then make a vertical cut starting at the bottom (6 o'clock), stopping 1cm before the goat's cheese. Repeat this at 3, 9 and 12 o'clock. Continue making evenly spaced cuts into the pastry until there are 32 in total. Brush the pastry border and just inside the goat's cheese ring with milk.

5 Starting at the bottom, fold one strip of pastry over the cheese to encase, then press to seal on the inside of the cheese circle. Working clockwise around the quiche, skip the next strip, then fold over the third one to seal in the cheese. Go back to strip 2, fold over and then move on to strip 4. Repeat folding alternate strips to make a filled pastry crust. Brush the top and sides of the crust with milk and chill for 30 minutes.

6 **Make the filling.** Meanwhile, heat the oven to 190°C/170°C fan/Gas 5. Drizzle the red peppers with the oil and roast them in a baking tin for 15 minutes, until softened. Add the spring onions and cook for a further 3–4 minutes, until softened. Leave to cool.

7 **Blind bake the case.** Meanwhile, line the chilled quiche case with baking paper and fill it with baking beans. Bake it for 15 minutes, until the pastry is just starting to turn golden at the edges. Remove the paper and beans.

8 **Assemble the quiche.** In a jug, whisk the eggs, yolks and cream, then season with salt and pepper. Arrange the roasted peppers, Peppadews, courgette and spring onions in the middle of the pastry and scatter with half the gruyère. Pour the egg mixture over, scatter with the remaining cheese and the chilli and bake for 30 minutes, until set and the pastry is crisp.

Autumn hedgerow tart

Serves 6–8
Hands on: 2 hours + chilling
Bake: 55 mins

FOR THE HAZELNUT PÂTE SUCRÉE
200g unsalted butter,
  cubed and softened
90g icing sugar, sifted
4 large egg yolks
1 tsp finely grated unwaxed
  lemon zest
370g plain flour
70g finely ground hazelnuts
1 egg white, lightly beaten

FOR THE FILLING
75g blanched hazelnuts
1 eating apple, peeled, cored,
  and chopped into small chunks
juice of 1 lemon
500g mixed autumn berries
  (such as 200g blackberries,
  200g elderberries,
  100g blackcurrants)
75g golden caster sugar
1 tbsp cornflour
2 tbsp sloe gin (optional)
double cream, to serve

FOR THE GLAZE
1 egg yolk
1 tbsp whole milk

You will need
23cm loose-bottomed fluted
  tart tin, lightly greased
baking beans
ruler
pizza wheel
autumnal-themed cutters,
  such as leaves, acorns
  and fruit

This autumnal recipe is one of my favourites, as it captures all the flavours of the season – and is visually impressive too. I love to wander up and down the little green lanes where I live, foraging berries and nuts to use in the filling.

1 **Make the hazelnut pâte sucrée.** Beat the butter and icing sugar in a stand mixer fitted with the beater, on medium speed for 2 minutes, scraping down the inside of the bowl from time to time, until pale and creamy. Add the egg yolks and lemon zest and mix to combine.

2 Add the flour and ground hazelnuts and mix again briefly on low speed until just combined, taking care not to overwork the dough. Tip the pastry onto the work surface and lightly knead for 20 seconds to bring it together into a neat ball. Cut the dough in half, flatten each piece into a disc, wrap and chill it for 1 hour.

3 Lightly flour the work surface and roll out one portion of the pastry into a 28cm disc, about 3mm thick and large enough to line the base and sides of the tart tin. Using a rolling pin, carefully lift the pastry into the tart tin (the dough will be quite soft but you can patch it up, if you need to). Gently press the pastry into the base and up the sides, taking care not to stretch it to avoid shrinkage during baking. Trim the excess pastry from the top with a sharp knife and prick the base of the pastry case with a fork, then chill for 30 minutes. Meanwhile, heat the oven to 180°C/160°C fan/Gas 4.

4 **Start the filling.** Tip the blanched hazelnuts into a small baking tin and toast them in the oven for 5 minutes. Leave them to cool slightly, then roughly chop them and set aside.

5 Line the pastry case with baking paper and fill it with baking beans. Bake for 12 minutes, or until the top edge of the pastry starts to turn golden. Remove the paper and beans, and lightly brush the base of the tart with egg white and return it to the oven for 3–4 minutes, until dry and sealed. Set aside to cool and turn off the oven until you're ready to bake the tart.

6 **Finish the filling.** Meanwhile, put the apple chunks in a bowl and sprinkle them with a little of the lemon juice to prevent them discolouring. In a separate bowl, mix the berries with the caster sugar, cornflour and the remaining lemon juice and set aside to macerate until needed.

7 **Prepare the pastry lid.** Roll the second piece of pastry into a 28cm disc, about 3mm thick. Using the ruler and pizza wheel, cut the pastry into 7–8mm-wide strips – you will need at least

Continues overleaf

Autumn hedgerow tart
continued

twenty. Gather the offcuts into a ball, re-roll it and use the autumnal cutters to stamp out leaves, acorns, apples or any other seasonally themed decorations.

8 **Fill the pie.** Mix the toasted chopped hazelnuts with the apple, berries and their juices and the sloe gin, if using, and spoon the filling into the cooled pastry case.

9 **Make the lattice.** Take one of the longest strips of pastry dough from the centre of the pastry disc and lay it vertically down the middle of the filled pie, then lay a slightly shorter strip either side, placing the strips close together. Counting from the left, fold strips one and three up back over themselves.

10 Take a second long strip of pastry and lay it horizontally across the middle. Fold strips one and three back down over the horizontal strip. Repeat this, placing a slightly shorter strip either side of the horizontal one, but this time picking up alternate strips – by now there should be three horizontal and three vertical strips. Keep the lattice even and neat, and the strips placed close together. Continue the lattice, alternating with horizontal and vertical strips until you reach the edges of the tart. Gently press the uncooked pastry lattice against the cooked tart case (taking care not to break it) and trim any uncooked pastry.

11 Heat the oven to 180°C/160°C fan/Gas 4. Position the pastry decorations all around the outside rim of the tart, covering the lattice joins and brushing them with a little water to stick them down. Arrange the leaves, or other decorations, around the lattice.

12 Mix the egg yolk with the milk and lightly brush the mixture all over the pastry lattice and decorations to glaze. Bake for 30–35 minutes, until the pastry is golden and the filling hot and bubbling. Leave to cool completely in the tin before removing and serving in slices, with double cream.

Lamb samosas

Makes: 24
Hands on: 2 hours + resting
Bake: 20 mins

FOR THE FILLING
3 banana shallots, finely chopped
2 garlic cloves, crushed
5cm piece of fresh ginger, grated
1 green chilli, finely chopped
1 tbsp olive oil
400g lamb mince
½ tsp ground coriander
½ tsp cumin seeds
½ tsp ground turmeric
½ tsp Kashmiri chilli powder
1 small cinnamon stick
1 tbsp tomato purée
1 tbsp tamarind paste
12 fresh, frozen or dried
    curry leaves
250ml lamb or vegetable stock
200g potato, peeled and diced
75g frozen peas
2 tbsp chopped coriander
salt and freshly ground
    black pepper

FOR THE PASTRY
250g plain flour
125g chickpea (gram) flour
½ tsp bicarbonate of soda
1 tsp medium curry powder
2 tsp nigella or black onion seeds
100ml sunflower or groundnut oil,
    plus extra for brushing
1 tsp white wine or cider vinegar

You will need
2 baking sheets, lined
    with baking paper

These lamb samosas are baked rather than fried, which makes them less fiddly to cook, but no less delicious. Prepare the filling the day before you plan on baking and serving the samosas to give the spices plenty of time to mellow.

. . . .

1 **Make the filling.** Place the shallots, garlic, ginger, chilli and olive oil in a pan. Cook on a low–medium heat for 2–3 minutes, stirring often, until soft and aromatic but not coloured. Turn the heat up to high, add the lamb to the pan and cook briefly, stirring to break up the mince, until browned. Stir in the spices and cook for another 30 seconds. Add the tomato purée, tamarind paste and curry leaves. Season well with salt and pepper, stir to combine, and cook for a further 1 minute.

2 Add the stock and potato to the pan, bring to the boil, then reduce the heat to a very gentle simmer and cover with the lid. Cook for 30 minutes, stirring frequently until the sauce has reduced and thickened. Add the peas (no need to defrost) and coriander, remove the pan from the heat and leave to cool. Remove the cinnamon stick, cover the filling and refrigerate it until you're ready to make the samosas.

3 **Make the pastry.** While the filling is cooling, sift the flour, chickpea flour, bicarbonate of soda and curry powder into a large bowl. Mix in the seeds and season with salt and pepper. Make a well in the middle of the dry ingredients, then add the oil, vinegar and 125ml of water. Mix to combine using a rubber spatula, then with your hands. Add a little more water if you need it to bring the dough together into a ball. Tip out the dough onto your work surface and knead it for 20 seconds, until smooth (take care not to overwork it). Return the dough to the bowl, cover and leave to rest for 40 minutes to 1 hour.

4 **Assemble the samosas.** Divide the rested dough into 12 equal balls (about 50g each), and cover half of them. Lightly flour the work surface and roll out six of the balls into neat discs, each 16–17cm in diameter. Take one disc and cut it in half. Lightly brush the straight edge of one piece of the dough with water and shape it into a cone, overlapping the edges and pressing to seal.

5 Spoon a dessertspoon of the curry filling into the cone, lightly brush one side of the open end with water and press the edges together to seal. Place the samosa on a lined baking sheet and repeat steps 4 and 5 to make 24 samosas in total.

6 **Bake the samosas.** Heat the oven to 190°C/170°C fan/Gas 5. Lightly brush the samosas with oil and bake for 20 minutes, until the pastry is crisp and golden, and the filling is piping hot. Serve warm with pickles, raita and chutneys.

Pear, hazelnut & chocolate tart

Serves: 8
Hands on: 1 hour + chilling
Bake: 1¼ hours

FOR THE PEARS
3 ripe pears, peeled
200g caster sugar
1 vanilla pod,
    split lengthways
juice of ½ lemon

FOR THE PASTRY
200g plain flour
pinch of salt
125g unsalted butter,
    cubed and chilled
40g icing sugar, sifted
1 egg, separated
2 tbsp ice-cold water
2 tsp lemon juice

FOR THE FRANGIPANE FILLING
AND TO DECORATE
100g blanched hazelnuts
50g plain flour
125g unsalted butter,
    cubed and softened
125g caster sugar
2 eggs, lightly beaten
1 tsp finely grated unwaxed
    lemon zest
1 tsp vanilla paste
50g ground almonds
½ tsp baking powder
pinch of salt
75g 70% dark chocolate, chopped

You will need
23cm loose-bottomed,
    fluted tart tin
heavy baking sheet
baking beans

The frangipane filling in this tart is made with hazelnuts (instead of the more usual almonds). The result is a heavenly combination of hazelnut, pears and chocolate.

· · · · · · · · · · · ·

1 **Poach the pears.** Put the pears, sugar, vanilla pod and lemon juice in a pan. Pour over about 700ml of water to cover the pears and bring the liquid to a gentle simmer on a low–medium heat, stirring to dissolve the sugar. Cover with a disc of baking paper, turn the heat to low and simmer the pears for 10 minutes, until just tender when tested with the point of a sharp knife. Remove from the heat and leave the pears to cool in the syrup.

2 **Make the pastry case.** Meanwhile, tip the flour and salt into a large bowl. Using your fingertips, rub in the butter until the mixture resembles breadcrumbs, with small, buttery flecks. Mix in the icing sugar, egg yolk, water and lemon juice with a table knife, then use your hands to gather the pastry into a ball. Flatten it into a disc, then wrap and chill it for 1 hour, until firm.

3 Flour the work surface and roll out the dough into a neat disc, 2–3mm thick. Use the disc to line the base and sides of the tin, trim any excess and chill for 20 minutes. Heat the oven to 180°C/160°C fan/Gas 4 with the heavy baking sheet on the middle shelf.

4 Prick the base of the pastry case, line it with baking paper and fill it with baking beans. Place it on top of the hot baking sheet and bake for 20 minutes, until the edges are pale golden. Remove the lining and beans, brush with egg white and bake for a further 10 minutes to cook the base. Remove from the oven (leave the baking sheet in place and the oven on) and leave to cool.

5 **Make the frangipane.** Finely grind 50g of the hazelnuts with 1 tablespoon of the flour in a mini food processor. Beat the butter and sugar in a stand mixer for about 3 minutes, until pale and creamy. A little at a time, beat in the eggs, scraping down the inside of the bowl occasionally. Mix in the lemon zest and vanilla. Beat in the ground hazelnuts, ground almonds, baking powder, salt and remaining flour until smooth. Spoon the frangipane into the pastry case and spread it level.

6 **Assemble the tart.** Remove the pears from the syrup. Cut them in half through the stalk and carefully scoop out the cores using a teaspoon. Pat the pear halves dry with kitchen paper and cut them into roughly 2–3cm-long wedges. Roughly chop the remaining 50g of hazelnuts and mix them with the chocolate. Scatter half the chocolate mixture over the frangipane and top with the pears. Scatter the remaining chocolate mixture between the pear slices, then bake the tart on the hot baking sheet for 45 minutes, until golden. Leave to cool.

5
Patisserie

Passion fruit & mango opera cake

Makes: 8
Hands on: 2 hours + chilling
Bake: 7 mins

FOR THE JOCONDE SPONGES
100g ground almonds
150g caster sugar
50g plain flour
3 eggs
1 tsp vanilla paste
25g unsalted butter, melted
3 egg whites
pinch of salt

FOR THE FRENCH BUTTERCREAM
6 egg yolks
150g caster sugar
200g unsalted butter,
    cubed and softened
1 tsp vanilla paste
150g good-quality white
    chocolate, chopped

FOR THE SYRUP
1 tbsp passion fruit purée
2 tbsp yuzu juice
25g caster sugar

FOR THE JELLY
4 platinum-grade gelatine leaves
200ml passion fruit purée
200ml canned Alphonso mango pulp
1 tbsp yuzu juice
edible flowers, to decorate

You will need
3 baking sheets, each lined with a
    piece of baking paper drawn with
    a 20cm square, drawn-side down
sugar thermometer
20cm square cake tin, greased,
    then lined (base and sides)
    with baking paper
ruler
small piping bag fitted with
    a medium open star nozzle

This showstopper of a cake is at its beautiful best if you make it ahead of serving, to allow the layers to set and the flavours to mingle. Avoid using fresh mango for the jelly, as the fresh fruit has an enzyme that prevents setting. Instead, use tinned Alphonso mango purée – not only will the jelly set, but the flavour is totally sublime.

. . . .

1 **Make the sponges.** Heat the oven to 200°C/180°C fan/Gas 6. Whisk the ground almonds, 100g of the sugar, and the flour, whole eggs and vanilla in a stand mixer fitted with the whisk, on medium speed for 1 minute, until pale. Add the melted butter and whisk again to combine.

2 In another large bowl, whisk the egg whites with the salt until they hold medium firm peaks. Add the remaining 50g of sugar and whisk for another 1 minute, until smooth and glossy. Using a large metal spoon or rubber spatula, fold the egg whites into the sponge mixture.

3 Carefully divide the mixture between the squares drawn on the sheets of baking paper, taking care not to lose any air. Using an offset palette knife, gently spread the mixture to fill each square and just cover the outlines. Bake for 7 minutes, until the sponges are set and just firm when pressed and starting to turn golden. Leave to cool on the baking paper.

4 **Make the French buttercream.** Whisk the egg yolks in a stand mixer fitted with the whisk, on medium speed for 1 minute, until slightly pale in colour. Meanwhile, bring the sugar and 80ml of water to the boil in a small pan on a low–medium heat until the sugar dissolves. Continue to boil until the syrup reaches 115°C on the sugar thermometer.

5 With the mixer running on low speed, add the hot syrup in a slow and steady stream to the egg yolks. Scrape down the inside of the bowl, increase the speed to medium and continue whisking for 2–3 minutes, until the mixture is pale and light, and holds a ribbon trail when you lift the whisk. It will have cooled to room temperature at this point.

6 A tablespoon at a time, add the butter, mixing on a low speed between each addition, until the butter is fully incorporated. Then, mix in the vanilla.

7 Meanwhile, melt the white chocolate in a heatproof bowl set over a pan of gently simmering water. Remove from the heat, stir until smooth and leave to cool for 3 minutes. Mix the cooled

Continues overleaf

Passion fruit & mango opera cake
continued

white chocolate into the buttercream. Set aside 2 tablespoons of the buttercream in a small bowl. Cover and set aside the rest of the buttercream.

8 **Make the syrup.** Mix all the syrup ingredients in a small pan and add 3 tablespoons of water. Bring to the boil, stirring until the sugar dissolves, then reduce the heat and simmer for 30 seconds to 1 minute. Leave to cool.

9 **Make the jelly.** Soak the gelatine leaves in a bowl of cold water for 5 minutes, until soft. Meanwhile, mix the passion fruit purée, mango pulp and yuzu juice in a jug with 100ml of water. Spoon half of the mixture into a small pan or microwave-safe bowl and heat until just bubbling. Strain the gelatine and squeeze out any excess moisture. Add the gelatine to the hot purée, whisk to melt and combine, then pour it back into the jug and whisk again. Set aside to cool, then cover and chill for 15 minutes, until the jelly starts to thicken.

10 **To assemble the cake.** Use the ruler to trim each sponge layer to a neat 20cm square. Place one sponge in the bottom of the tin and brush it with a third of the passion fruit syrup. Using a palette knife, spread half of the buttercream evenly on top using an offset palette knife. Cover with the second sponge layer and brush with another third of the syrup. Chill the stacked sponges for 20 minutes.

11 When chilled, spoon half (about 250ml) of the cooled jelly on top of the second sponge in an even layer and chill for another 30 minutes. Cover the jelly with the third sponge, brush with the remaining syrup and spoon over the rest of the buttercream, spreading it level. Chill for 2 hours, until firm.

12 Slightly warm the remaining jelly if it has set; it should be just warm enough to pour, but not hot. Pour the jelly on top of the buttercream in an even layer and chill the cake for at least 4 hours, until set.

13 Spoon the reserved 2 tablespoons of buttercream into the small piping bag fitted with the medium open star nozzle. Lift the cake out of the tin and, using a warmed long-bladed knife, trim the sides and cut the cake into 8 even-sized rectangles. Pipe a rosette of buttercream on top of each slice and decorate with edible flowers to serve.

Gâteau Concorde

Serves: 8
Hands on: 1½ hours
   + cooling and chilling
Bake: 1 hour

FOR THE MERINGUE
5 egg whites (about 175g; save
   4 yolks for the mousseline)
pinch of cream of tartar
pinch of salt
225g caster sugar
125g icing sugar, plus extra
   for dusting
30g cocoa powder

FOR THE MOUSSELINE
150g 70% dark chocolate, chopped
100g caster sugar
500ml double cream
pinch of sea-salt flakes
4 egg yolks

FOR THE CHOCOLATE CURLS
75g 70% dark chocolate, chopped

You will need
18cm-diameter plate or cake tin,
   as a template
2 large baking sheets, each lined
   with a sheet of baking paper
large piping bag fitted with
   a medium plain nozzle
20cm springform tin, base-lined
   with baking paper
65 x 8cm acetate strip

The original Gâteau Concorde was served to passengers on board the Concorde aeroplane. This updated version has a rich, salted caramel mousseline filling, which makes good use of the egg yolks left over from making the meringue. Serve it on the day you assemble, otherwise the meringue will soften.

. . . .

1 Heat the oven to 120°C/100°C fan/Gas ¾. Using the 18cm plate or cake tin as a guide, draw two 18cm circles on one sheet of baking paper lining one of the baking sheets, and a third 18cm circle on the other sheet of baking paper. Turn both sheets so that the circles are drawn-side down.

2 **Make the meringue.** Whisk the egg whites with the cream of tartar and salt in a stand mixer fitted with the whisk, on medium–high speed until the egg whites form soft peaks. Add the caster sugar, 1 tablespoon at a time, whisking well between each addition and scraping down the inside of the bowl from time to time, until the meringue is smooth and glossy, with no granules of sugar. Sift the icing sugar and cocoa powder into the bowl and fold them in using a rubber spatula or large metal spoon.

3 Spoon the meringue into the large piping bag fitted with the plain nozzle. Pipe three discs of the meringue onto the baking paper, using the templates as a guide and starting from the middle of the circles and working outwards. Pipe the remaining meringue into 12 long, thin pencils, about 20cm in length, alongside the discs. Bake the meringues for 1 hour, until cooked and crisp. Leave the meringues to cool in the oven for at least 2 hours, without opening the door.

4 **Make the mousseline.** Melt the chocolate in a heatproof bowl set over a pan of gently simmering water, stir until smooth, then remove from the heat.

5 Meanwhile, tip half of the caster sugar into a small pan, add 1 tablespoon of water and place the pan on a low heat to dissolve the sugar, swirling the pan occasionally. Bring to the boil and cook until the syrup becomes an amber-coloured caramel, swirling the pan to ensure the caramel cooks evenly. Slide the pan off the heat and gradually stir in 100ml of the double cream and the sea-salt flakes, then return the pan to a low heat to melt any hardened caramel. Using a rubber spatula, scoop the caramel into a bowl and set aside.

6 Tip the remaining sugar into the same pan (no need to wash it) and add 2 tablespoons of water. Place over a low heat, stirring to

Continues overleaf

Gâteau Concorde

continued

dissolve the sugar, then bring to the boil and simmer for 1 minute, until the syrup has reduced and thickened slightly.

7 Using an electric hand whisk or a balloon whisk, beat the egg yolks in a large heatproof bowl until combined, then pour in the hot syrup, whisking continuously and scraping down the inside of the bowl. Set the bowl over a pan of gently simmering water and continue to whisk for 2 minutes, until the mixture is thick and pale, and holds a ribbon trail when you lift the whisk. Remove the bowl from the heat and whisk for a further 2–3 minutes, until the mixture has cooled. Whisk in the salted caramel, then fold in the melted chocolate.

8 Whisk the remaining 400ml of double cream to soft peaks. Fold one-third of the cream into the chocolate mixture to loosen, then add the remaining cream in two batches, folding it in gently with a rubber spatula or large metal spoon.

9 **Assemble the meringue cake.** Line the sides of the springform tin with the acetate strip. Place one meringue layer in the tin and spread a quarter of the chocolate mousseline over the top. Repeat this layering, finishing with the third meringue layer. Chill for 1 hour, until set and firmed up. Cover the remaining mousseline and leave it at room temperature.

10 **Make the chocolate curls.** Meanwhile, melt the chocolate for the curls as before, stir until smooth and remove from the heat. Pour the melted chocolate over the underside of a flat baking sheet and spread it level until 3mm thick. Sharply tap the baking sheet on the work surface to level the chocolate and to burst any air bubbles. Chill the chocolate for 15 minutes, until set but not solid.

11 Using a kitchen knife, hold the blade firmly at a 45-degree angle to the chocolate and push it across the top of the chocolate to create curls. Place the curls on a baking tray and chill until you're ready to use.

12 **Assemble the gâteau.** Remove the meringue cake from the tin, peel off the acetate collar and place it on a serving plate. Cover the top and sides of the cake with the remaining chocolate mousseline, spreading it smoothly and evenly with an offset palette knife.

13 Cut the meringue pencils to the same height as the meringue cake and arrange them upright around the outside of the cake. You can pile any remaining pieces onto the top of the cake. Arrange the chocolate curls on top of the cake, then finish with a dusting of icing sugar.

Croissants with praline crème pâtissière

Makes: 8
Hands on: 1½ hours + proving
   (including overnight)
Bake: 25 mins

FOR THE CROISSANT DOUGH
280g strong white bread flour
30g caster sugar
1 tsp salt
7g fast-action dried yeast
85ml whole milk
vegetable oil, for greasing
200g unsalted butter
   (as a block), chilled
1 egg, beaten

FOR THE PRALINE
120g whole blanched hazelnuts
120g blanched almonds
160g caster sugar
1–2 tsp hazelnut oil

FOR THE CRÈME PÂTISSIÈRE
50g caster sugar
2 large egg yolks
20g cornflour
250ml whole milk
½ tsp vanilla paste (optional)

You will need
ruler
2 baking sheets, lined
   with baking paper
2 proving bags
baking sheet, lined
   with a silicone sheet
medium piping bag fitted
   with a jam nozzle

I first tried these croissants when visiting my Grandad in Spain. Now, they have become a Christmas morning family tradition – I do all the hard work on Christmas eve so that we all have a delicious breakfast to wake up to.

● ● ● ● ● ● ● ● ● ●

1 **Make the croissant dough.** Mix the flour, sugar, salt, yeast and milk with 85ml of water in a stand mixer fitted with the dough hook, on medium speed for 8–10 minutes, until the dough is smooth and elastic. Place the dough in an oiled bowl, cover and leave to prove at room temperature for at least 1 hour, until tripled in size.

2 Knead the dough gently for 30 seconds to knock it back, shape it roughly into a rectangle, then wrap it and leave it to prove overnight in the fridge or for at least 12 hours.

3 While the dough is proving, place the block of chilled butter between two sheets of baking paper and tap it with the end of a rolling pin to flatten it into a 15cm square. Keep the butter wrapped in the baking paper and place it in the fridge to chill with the dough, until firm.

4 **Roll the croissant dough.** Remove the dough and butter from the fridge and set the butter aside to soften slightly while you roll out the dough. The butter must be pliable and warm enough not to crack, but cool enough not to melt when you roll it out.

5 Lightly flour the work surface and roll out the dough to a rectangle, about 30 x 15cm. Place the square of butter in the middle of the dough and fold each side of the dough over to meet in the middle of the butter and cover it. Pinch the edges of the dough together to seal.

6 Roll out the dough (with the butter sealed inside) away from you into a rectangle, about 45 x 15cm, with one of the short sides closest to you. Brush off any excess flour, then fold the bottom third of the dough up to cover the middle third and fold the top third down on top so that you have three neat layers, and a seam of dough facing you. Give it a quick light roll to compress and even out the surface, then wrap and chill for 1 hour.

7 Place the dough back on the floured work surface with the seam facing you, then rotate it 90° clockwise so that the seam is now on the left. Repeat the rolling out and folding from the previous step and chill for 1 hour. Remove the dough from the fridge and repeat the rolling, folding and chilling again.

Continues overleaf

Croissants with praline crème pâtissière
continued

8 Cut the dough pieces. Once the dough has chilled a final time, roll it out on a floured work surface as neatly as possible into a rectangle, about 40 x 28cm. It's best to roll it out slightly larger, then trim it to size to remove any uneven edges.

9 Divide one of the long sides of the rectangle into 8cm lengths, marking each point with a small cut. Repeat on the opposite side, but making the first mark at 4cm, then the rest at 8cm, so the cuts on either side are staggered. Once you have marked the points on the dough, use a large sharp knife and ruler to cut it into eight triangles, using the marks as the start and end points.

10 Shape the croissants. Take the first triangle of dough and gently stretch it out to make it slightly longer. Place the stretched triangle on the work surface and make a small cut in the middle of the triangle base. Starting with that side, roll up the dough into a croissant, shaping it slightly into a crescent.

11 Repeat Step 10 to make eight croissants in total, placing them on the lined baking sheets with the pointed end of the triangle tucked underneath as you go. Slide the baking sheets into the proving bags and leave the croissants to prove for 1–3 hours (depending on the temperature of the room), until doubled in size and they wobble slightly when you nudge the trays.

12 Bake the croissants. When the croissants are almost ready, heat the oven to 210°C/190°C fan/Gas 6–7. Gently brush them with the beaten egg, taking care not to deflate them. Bake for 10 minutes, then turn the oven down to 190°C/170°C fan/Gas 5 and bake for a further 15 minutes, until golden brown. Transfer the croissants to a wire rack to cool completely.

13 Make the praline. While the croissants are cooling, heat the oven to 200°C/180°C fan/Gas 6. Place the hazelnuts and almonds into the lined baking tray and toast in the oven for 10–15 minutes, until golden, then leave to cool.

14 Tip the sugar into a heavy-based pan. Add 3 tablespoons of water and heat on a high heat until the sugar dissolves and turns to a dark amber colour, swirling the pan occasionally. Remove the pan from the heat and carefully stir in the toasted nuts with a wooden spoon, then pour the mixture onto the baking sheet lined with the silicone sheet and leave to cool and harden.

15 Break the cooled caramel into pieces and place it in a mini food processor. Add 1 teaspoon of the hazelnut oil, then blitz to a smooth, buttery paste, scraping down the inside of the processor bowl from time to time. Add a splash more oil if the paste is too thick. Transfer the paste to a separate bowl, cover it and set aside until you're ready to use. (This makes more praline than you need, but it will keep in a sealed container for up to 3 months.)

16 **Make the crème pâtissière.** In a large bowl, using a balloon whisk, whisk the sugar with the egg yolks, cornflour and 1 tablespoon of the milk, until pale and combined.

17 Gently heat the remaining milk in a small pan with the vanilla, if using, until it just comes to the boil. Pour the hot milk into the egg mixture and whisk until well combined. Return the mixture to the pan and heat gently, whisking continuously, until it thickens to a custard consistency. Pour the crème into a bowl, cover with a disc of baking paper and leave to cool, then chill until set.

18 **Fill the croissants.** Once the crème pâtissière has set, fold through 2 tablespoons of the praline paste. Spoon the mixture into the piping bag fitted with the jam nozzle. Pierce a hole in the base of each croissant the same size as the tip of the nozzle, then pipe the crème through the hole to fill the croissant. You will have to move the piping tip around slightly to fill each end and to ensure the croissants are evenly filled. Repeat to fill all eight croissants.

Ginger financiers

Makes: 12
Hands on: 20 mins
Bake: 20 mins

125g unsalted butter, cubed
125g icing sugar, sifted
50g caster sugar
50g plain flour
3 tsp ground ginger
½ tsp ground cardamom
pinch of freshly grated nutmeg
125g ground almonds
pinch of salt
1 tsp finely grated unwaxed
    lemon zest
5 egg whites
3 balls of stem ginger in syrup,
    drained, finely chopped
25g flaked almonds
2 tbsp stem ginger syrup

TO DECORATE
2 tsp lemon juice,
    plus extra if needed
2 tbsp icing sugar, sifted,
    plus extra if needed
1 tbsp edible gold balls
1 tbsp finely chopped candied
    stem ginger (optional)

You will need
12-hole mini-loaf tin, greased
small piping bag fitted with a
    small writing nozzle (optional)

Financiers are a petite, classic French cake, baked to resemble little gold bars. They are perfect to serve with coffee. Browned butter gives a natural nuttiness to the sponges, which pairs beautifully with the ginger and other warming spices.

. . . .

1 **Make the sponges.** Heat the butter in a small saucepan on a low–medium heat, occasionally swirling the pan, until the milk solids turn golden brown and caramelise, and the butter smells nutty. Pour the brown butter into a small bowl and leave to cool.

2 Heat the oven to 170°C/150°C fan/Gas 3.

3 Sift both sugars, and the flour, spices, ground almonds and salt into a large bowl, add the lemon zest and make a well in the middle of the dry ingredients.

4 In another bowl, whisk the egg whites until foamy, then add them to the dry ingredients. Using a silicone spatula, beat everything together until smooth. Add the brown butter in three batches, mixing each batch until smooth and thoroughly combined, then fold in the stem ginger to evenly distribute.

5 Divide the mixture equally between the holes in the prepared tin, level the tops and scatter with the flaked almonds. Bake on the middle shelf for 20 minutes, until risen and golden, and a skewer inserted into the centre of each cake comes out clean.

6 Leave the cakes to cool in the tin for 2 minutes, then carefully remove them to a wire rack. Brush the top of each financier with the stem ginger syrup and leave to cool.

7 **Decorate the financiers.** Whisk together the lemon juice and icing sugar to make a drizzly, runny icing, adding more sugar or juice as needed. Using a teaspoon (or small piping bag), drizzle the icing over the top of each financier in a zig-zag pattern, then scatter with the edible gold balls and candied ginger, if using. Leave the icing to set before serving.

Prue's tarte aux pommes

Serves: 10
Hands on: 1 hour + chilling
Bake: 55 mins

FOR THE PÂTE BRISÉE
250g plain flour
½ tsp salt
150g unsalted butter,
    cubed and chilled
1 large egg, separated
2–3 tbsp ice-cold water

FOR THE APPLE PURÉE
600g (about 6 small) eating apples,
    preferably Cox, peeled, cored
    and cut into 1cm pieces
juice of 1 lemon
30g unsalted butter

FOR THE LEMON SYRUP
100g caster sugar
juice of 1 lemon

FOR THE FRANGIPANE
50g unsalted butter,
    softened and cubed
50g caster sugar
1 large egg
70g ground almonds
2 tbsp calvados

FOR THE TOPPING
4 large red-skinned eating apples,
    cored, halved, and cut into
    3mm thin slices
15g unsalted butter, melted

FOR THE APRICOT GLAZE
3 apricots, stoned and roughly
    chopped into 1cm pieces
50g jam sugar

You will need
25cm loose-bottomed
    sandwich or tart tin
baking beans

There are as many versions of this classic of French patisserie as there are cheeses! For this version, Prue has added calvados to the frangipane and put the filling in a pâte brisée shell, for its crumbly, buttery texture.

· · · · · · · · · ·

1 **Make the pâte brisée.** Tip the flour and salt into a bowl. Rub the butter into the flour mixture with your fingertips until it resembles breadcrumbs. Make a well in the middle, add the egg yolk (reserving the white) and 2 tablespoons of the ice-cold water. Using a table knife, bring the mixture together to form a dough, adding the extra 1 tablespoon of water if needed.

2 Lightly flour the work surface, tip the pastry out of the bowl and shape the dough into a ball, then wrap and chill it for 20 minutes.

3 **Make the apple purée.** While the pâte brisée is chilling, tip the apples into a pan, add the lemon juice and butter, then simmer for 20 minutes, until the apples are soft and any liquid has evaporated. Remove from the heat and crush the apples with a potato masher or wooden spoon to a coarse purée. Leave to cool.

4 **Make the pastry case.** Roll out the pâte brisée on a lightly floured work surface to a 30cm round and use the round to line the tart tin. Chill for 20 minutes.

5 Heat the oven to 180°C/160°C fan/Gas 4. Line the pastry case with baking paper and baking beans and bake blind for 20 minutes. Meanwhile, whisk the reserved egg white with a fork. Remove the baking beans and paper and brush the inside of the case with the egg white. Return the case to the oven and bake for 10 minutes to dry out the base. Leave to cool. Turn the oven off for now.

6 **Make the lemon syrup.** Pour 100ml of water into a pan, add the sugar and lemon juice and bring to the boil. Reduce the heat and simmer for 2–3 minutes, until the sugar dissolves. Pour the syrup into a large bowl and leave to cool slightly.

7 **Make the frangipane.** Beat the butter and sugar in a stand mixer fitted with the beater, on medium speed for 3–5 minutes, until pale and creamy. Add the egg and mix until combined. Turn the speed to low, add the ground almonds and calvados and mix until just combined; do not overmix.

8 Spoon the cold apple purée into the pastry case and level it with a palette knife, then spoon blobs of the frangipane on top and spread it out into an even layer.

Continues overleaf

Prue's tarte aux pommes
continued

9 **Make the topping.** Reheat the oven to 180°C/160°C fan/Gas 4. Place the apple slices in the warm lemon syrup and turn to coat. Working from the outside edge of the pastry case, dab each apple slice on kitchen paper to remove any excess syrup and arrange the slices in concentric overlapping circles. When you reach the middle, slice a few of the apple slices in half so they are wafer thin and shape them into an open rose to fill the hole in the centre of the tart. Brush all the apple slices with the melted butter and bake for 30 minutes.

10 **Make the apricot glaze.** Crush the apricots and jam sugar together in a small pan using the potato masher, then place the pan on a low heat. Leave the fruit and sugar to slump and then increase the heat slightly to bring the mixture to the boil. Immediately reduce the heat again to a strong simmer, and cook for 4 minutes, until you have a jammy consistency. Remove from the heat and pass the mixture through a fine-mesh sieve. Stir 2 tablespoons of water into the purée to give a thin glaze.

11 Remove the tart from the oven, leave it to cool for 5 minutes, then brush the top with the apricot glaze.

Rhubarb & custard mille feuille

Makes: 10
Hands on: 3 hours + chilling
Bake: 1–1½ hours

FOR THE PUFF PASTRY
175g plain flour
125g strong white bread flour
pinch of salt
300g unsalted butter, chilled
125ml ice-cold water
1 tsp lemon juice
2 tbsp icing sugar, sifted

FOR THE RHUBARB
800g forced rhubarb,
    cut into 9cm lengths
150g caster sugar
juice of ½ large orange
½ vanilla pod, split

FOR THE CUSTARD
600ml whole milk
½ vanilla pod, split
6 egg yolks
125g caster sugar
50g cornflour
2 platinum-grade gelatine leaves
50g unsalted butter, cubed

FOR THE FILLING
200ml double cream
2 tbsp icing sugar, sifted

You will need
2 or 4 baking sheets,
    lined with baking paper
20cm square baking tin, lined
    (base and sides) with baking
    paper that overhangs the sides

In late winter or early spring, when forced pink rhubarb is at its colourful and flavourful best, these 'thousand-layered', flaky pastries are pretty enough for any patisserie window and taste utterly sublime.

. . . .

1 **Make the pastry.** Add both types of flour and the salt to a large bowl. Cut 50g of the butter into cubes and rub it into the flour until the mixture resembles breadcrumbs. Add the water and lemon juice and mix with a table knife to bring the dough together. Add a little extra water if needed. Gather the pastry into a ball, then flatten it into a neat postcard-size rectangle. Wrap and it chill for 1 hour, until firm.

2 Lightly flour the work surface and roll out the pastry to a rectangle three times as long as it is wide (about 36 x 12cm), with one of the short sides nearest you. Cut the remaining 250g butter into 2cm-thick slices. Place the slices side-by-side between two sheets of baking paper and flatten and roll the butter with a rolling pin into a neat 11cm square, slightly smaller than one-third of the pastry rectangle. Place the butter on the middle section of the pastry and fold the bottom third up over it, brushing off any excess flour, then fold the top third down and lightly press the pastry edges together to seal in the butter.

3 Turn the pastry square 90° clockwise and roll it out again into a 36 x 12cm rectangle. Try to keep the pastry edges as neat as possible. As before, fold the bottom third of the pastry rectangle up over the middle third and the top third down, brushing off any excess flour. Lightly press the pastry edges together, turn the square 90° clockwise, then wrap and chill it for 45 minutes.

4 Roll out the pastry again, as in Step 3, and fold it again into neat thirds. Then, finally, roll the dough into a neat rectangle three times as long as it is wide, and this time fold the top edge down to the middle and the bottom edge up to the middle to meet it. Turn the dough 90° clockwise on the work surface, then fold it in half like closing a book. Wrap and chill the pastry for at least 2 hours.

5 **Bake the rhubarb.** Meanwhile, heat the oven to 180°C/160°C fan/Gas 4. Place the rhubarb in a large ovenproof dish. Add the sugar, orange juice and vanilla pod and turn until combined. Spread out the rhubarb in an even layer, cover the dish with foil and bake for 15 minutes, until the fruit is tender but still holds its shape. Leave to cool, then chill until you're ready to assemble.

6 **Make the custard.** Heat the milk with the vanilla pod until just boiling, then remove it from the heat. In a large bowl, whisk the

Continues overleaf

Rhubarb & custard mille feuille
continued

egg yolks, sugar and cornflour until combined. Pour half of the hot milk into the bowl, whisking continuously until smooth. Return the mixture to the pan and cook on a low–medium heat, whisking continuously until the custard starts to bubble, thicken and the cornflour has been cooked out. Remove the pan from the heat and strain the custard into a clean bowl.

7 In another bowl, soak the gelatine leaves in a bowl of cold water for 5 minutes, until soft and floppy. Drain the gelatine, squeeze out the excess water, then whisk it into the hot custard with the butter, until combined. Cover the surface of the custard with a piece of baking paper and leave to cool.

8 Cut the pastry into three equal-sized pieces. Lightly flour the work surface and roll each piece into a 25cm square, about 2–3mm thick. Slide each pastry square onto a sheet of baking paper, stack the sheets on top of one another, and chill the squares for 30 minutes.

9 Heat the oven to 200°C/180°C fan/Gas 6. Lift one pastry square, on its paper, onto a lined baking sheet. Prick the pastry with a fork, dust it with icing sugar and cover with another piece of baking paper. Top with a second baking sheet and bake the pastry for 25 minutes, until golden and starting to crisp. Remove the baking sheet and paper from the top of the pastry square and cook for a further 5 minutes, until golden, flaky and crisp. If you have four baking sheets you can cook two pastry squares at a time; if not, cook the pastry in batches, allowing the trays to cool down each time. Leave the baked pastry sheets to cool.

10 **Assemble the mille feuille.** Use the square baking tin as a template and cut each pastry sheet into a neat 20cm square. Carefully remove the rhubarb from the dish, saving the cooking juices, and place the rhubarb on kitchen paper to dry.

11 Whip the cream for the filling with the icing sugar and 2 tablespoons of the rhubarb juice to stiff peaks.

12 Place one pastry square in the bottom of the lined tin and spread it with half of the cold custard. Arrange half of the rhubarb neatly on top of the custard and spread it with half of the cream. Repeat this layering, finishing with the third pastry sheet, then gently press everything together. Cover and chill for 1–2 hours to firm up.

13 Using the lining paper, lift the filled pastry from the tin and, using a bread knife, cut it into 10 neat rectangles to serve.

Pain Suisse

Makes: 10
Hands on: 1 hour
  + overnight rising
Bake: 20 mins

FOR THE DOUGH
150g strong white bread flour
150g plain flour
5g fast-action dried yeast
25g caster sugar
½ tsp salt
100ml whole milk, lukewarm
2 eggs, lightly beaten
1 tsp vanilla paste
100g unsalted butter,
    cubed and softened
1 egg beaten with 1 tbsp
    whole milk, to glaze

FOR THE CRÈME PÂTISSIÈRE
250ml whole milk
3 egg yolks
50g light muscovado sugar
25g cornflour
1 tsp vanilla paste
pinch of salt

FOR THE FILLING AND TO FINISH
150g dark chocolate chips
50g dark chocolate, chopped

You will need
2 baking sheets, lined
    with baking paper

Made using traditional brioche dough, these Viennoiserie breakfast treats fall decadently somewhere between a pain au raisin and a pain au chocolat. Your mornings will never be the same again!

. . . .

1 **Make the dough.** Using a balloon whisk, whisk both types of flour, and the yeast, caster sugar and salt in the bowl of a stand mixer. Attach the bowl to the mixer fitted with the dough hook and make a well.

2 Add the warm milk, eggs and vanilla to the bowl and mix on low until combined. Scrape down the bowl and mix for 2–3 minutes, to a smooth dough. Gradually add the butter, mixing continuously for another 2 minutes, until the dough is silky smooth, elastic and cleanly leaves the sides of the bowl. Scrape down the bowl again, cover and leave the dough to rise overnight in the fridge.

3 **Make the crème pâtissière.** While the dough is rising, bring the milk to the boil in a small pan, then remove from the heat. Using a balloon whisk, beat the remaining crème pât ingredients in a bowl until pale. Whisk half of the hot milk onto the egg-yolk mixture, until smooth. Return the mixture to the pan and cook on a low–medium heat, stirring, for 1 minute, until the custard boils and thickens. Strain the custard into a clean bowl, cover the surface with baking paper, cool, then chill until needed.

4 **Assemble the pain Suisse.** Lightly flour the work surface and turn out the risen dough. Roll the dough (it will be springy, so roll a little, then rest, then roll) into a neat 45 x 30cm rectangle, with a long side nearest you.

5 Beat the chilled crème pât until smooth. Spread it over the bottom half of the dough, leaving a 1cm border at the bottom. Scatter with the chocolate chips. Fold the top of the dough down to cover the filling and press the edges to seal. Trim to neaten, then cut the dough vertically into 10 strips, each about 4–5cm wide. Arrange these on the lined baking sheets, cover loosely and leave to rise for 1½ hours, until nearly doubled in size.

6 Heat the oven to 180°C/160°C fan/Gas 4. Brush the dough with the egg wash and bake for 15–20 minutes, until risen and golden. Leave to cool.

7 Melt the chopped chocolate in a heatproof bowl set over a pan of gently simmering water. Stir until smooth and remove from the heat. Drizzle the chocolate over the top of the pain Suisse and leave to set before serving.

Summer berry charlotte

Serves: 8
Hands on: 2 hours + chilling
Bake: 20 mins

FOR THE SPONGE FINGERS
2 eggs, separated
1 tsp vanilla paste
60g caster sugar,
    plus extra for dusting
pinch of salt
50g plain flour, sifted

FOR THE GENOISE SPONGE
2 eggs
60g caster sugar
60g plain flour
10g unsalted butter, melted

FOR THE BAVAROIS
140g redcurrants
140g strawberries
340g raspberries
5 platinum-grade gelatine leaves
175ml whole milk
1 tsp vanilla paste
5 egg yolks
150g caster sugar
3 tbsp Chambord raspberry
    liqueur (optional)
350ml double cream

FOR THE TOPPING
1 platinum-grade gelatine leaf
fresh berries, to decorate
icing sugar, for dusting

You will need
ruler
large baking sheet, lined
    with a sheet of baking paper
large piping bag fitted with
    a medium plain nozzle
20cm sandwich tins x 2, greased,
    then base-lined with baking paper
20cm springform tin, greased, then
    base-lined with baking paper
65 x 8cm acetate strip

This classic dessert is perfect to make in the height of summer when fresh berries are sweet and in abundance. The clever technique for the sponge fingers fuses them together as they bake, so that they form a neat collar.

· · · · · · · · · · · ·

1 Draw two sets of parallel lines, each line 35cm long and spaced 7cm apart and with a 5cm gap between each set, on the baking paper lining the baking sheet. Place the paper drawn-side down.

2 **Make the sponge fingers.** Heat the oven to 190°C/170°C fan/ Gas 5. Using an electric hand whisk, whisk the egg yolks with the vanilla and 30g of the caster sugar, on medium speed until pale and the mixture leaves a ribbon trail when you lift the whisk. In a separate bowl, whisk the egg whites with the salt to soft, floppy peaks. A third at a time, whisk in the remaining sugar, whisking continuously until the egg whites form stiff but not dry peaks.

3 Using a large metal spoon, fold one-third of the meringue into the egg yolks, then fold in the sifted flour until almost combined. Fold in the remaining meringue in two batches.

4 Spoon the sponge finger batter into the piping bag fitted with the plain nozzle. Pipe two sets of 7cm-long biscuits onto the baking paper, using the parallel lines as a guide for length and leaving a 2–3mm gap between each (as the biscuits bake, they will join together into a long strip). The mixture should make about 45 finger biscuits in total. Sprinkle the biscuits with caster sugar and bake for 9 minutes, until just crisp and pale golden. Remove from the oven and leave to cool. Leave the oven on.

5 **Make the genoise sponge.** Whisk the eggs and sugar in a stand mixer fitted with the whisk, on medium speed for 3–4 minutes, until pale, doubled in volume, and the mixture leaves a ribbon trail when you lift the whisk. Sift in the flour and fold it in using a large metal spoon. Pour the melted butter around the inside edge of the bowl and fold in. Divide the mixture equally between the two 20cm cake tins and spread it level. Bake on the middle shelf for 8 minutes, until risen and golden, and the cakes spring back when pressed lightly with a fingertip. Leave to cool in the tin.

6 **Make the bavarois.** Tip the redcurrants, strawberries and 140g of the raspberries into a pan and cook on a low–medium heat for 2 minutes, stirring occasionally until the berries burst and are juicy. Remove from the heat, purée the fruit in a blender until almost smooth, then pass it through a fine-mesh sieve to remove the seeds. Measure out 100ml of the purée and set aside.

Continues overleaf

Summer berry charlotte
continued

7 Soak the gelatine leaves in a bowl of cold water for 5 minutes, until soft and floppy. Meanwhile, heat the milk with the vanilla on a medium heat until just boiling. Whisk the egg yolks with the caster sugar in a separate large bowl until combined.

8 Pour half of the hot milk onto the egg-yolk mixture, whisking continuously until smooth, then return it to the pan and whisk to combine. Cook on a low heat, stirring continuously until the custard thickens enough to coat the back of the spoon, but do not let it boil or the eggs may scramble, then strain into a clean bowl.

9 Drain the gelatine, squeezing it to remove any excess water, then add it to the custard and whisk until smooth and melted. Leave the custard to cool for 10 minutes, then stir in the larger portion of berry purée and leave it to cool completely. Chill for 15 minutes, until the bavarois just starts to thicken.

10 **Assemble the charlotte.** Meanwhile, line the sides of the springform tin with the acetate strip. Using an 18cm plate or tin as a guide, cut each genoise sponge into a neat disc and place one sponge in the bottom of the tin on top of the baking paper.

11 Slice one rounded end from each strip of sponge fingers and arrange the biscuits, cut-side down and top facing outwards, neatly around the inside edge of the tin against the acetate. Place the ends of each strip tightly together to prevent any of the filling escaping. If the biscuits have baked perfectly, they should line the circumference of the tin with no gaps.

12 Brush the genoise sponge in the tin with Chambord, if using, and scatter over half the remaining raspberries. Whip the cream to soft peaks and fold it into the chilled berry bavarois mixture to combine. Carefully spoon half of the bavarois into the lined tin and spread level with a palette knife. Top with the second genoise sponge layer and repeat with the Chambord, if using, and the remaining raspberries and bavarois. Chill for 1 hour, until set.

13 **Make the topping.** Soak the gelatine in cold water for 5 minutes, until soft and floppy. Heat half of the reserved berry purée in a small pan until hot but not boiling, then remove from the heat. Drain the gelatine and squeeze out any excess water, then add it to the pan and mix it through until melted and thoroughly combined. Add the remaining purée and mix to combine. Leave to cool, then pour the topping over the bavarois in an even layer. Chill for 1 hour, until set.

14 To serve, remove the charlotte from the tin, peel off the acetate strip and baking paper and place on a serving plate. Top with fresh berries and dust with icing sugar.

6
Dessert

Paul's ginger & orange treacle puddings

These individual puddings are laced with homemade golden syrup and steamed in the oven, rather than on the hob, making them a perfect end to a Sunday lunch – just pop them in to bake once you've finished the roasties.

· · · · · · · · · · ·

Makes: 6
Hands on: 40 mins + drying
Bake: 45 mins

FOR THE SYRUP
130g caster sugar
65ml just-boiled water
1 lemon wedge, about 2cm wide

FOR THE CRYSTALLISED ORANGE
1 unwaxed orange
100g caster sugar, plus
    extra for sprinkling

FOR THE SPONGE
175g unsalted butter,
    cubed and softened
175g caster sugar
3 eggs, beaten
185g self-raising flour
1 tsp ground ginger
3 balls of stem ginger in syrup,
    rinsed and finely chopped
2 tbsp ginger syrup from the
    stem ginger, to serve

FOR THE CRÈME ANGLAISE
125ml whole milk
125ml double cream
½ vanilla pod, seeds scraped out
3 egg yolks
30g caster sugar

You will need
200ml pudding basins x 6,
    greased, then base-lined with
    a greased round of baking paper
6 chopsticks or thick wooden skewers
6 circles of baking paper and 6 circles
    of foil cut 3cm larger than the
    top of the pudding basins
kitchen string

1 **Make the syrup.** Heat 30g of the sugar with 2 tablespoons of water on a low heat, stirring to dissolve. Increase the heat to medium and cook for 3–5 minutes to a golden caramel. Remove from the heat and pour in the just-boiled water. Add the lemon wedge and the remaining sugar, return the pan to the heat and stir until the mixture comes to the boil. Simmer gently on a low heat for 20 minutes, until light golden and syrupy. Cool, then divide the syrup between the pudding basins.

2 **Make the crystallised orange.** Using a potato peeler, peel a long, 3cm-wide strip from around the middle of the orange. Finely grate the remaining zest and set aside. Cut the long strip of peel into six 5mm-wide strips. Place the strips in a pan with the sugar and 100ml of water. Bring to the boil over a medium–high heat to dissolve the sugar, then simmer for 15 minutes, until translucent and tender. Drain the strips, reserving the syrup, and cool on a wire rack. Once cool enough to handle, wind each strip around a chopstick or skewer to create a spiral. Sprinkle with sugar and leave in a warm place for 1 hour to crystallise.

3 **Make the sponge.** Heat the oven to 180°C/160°C fan/Gas 4. Beat the butter and sugar in a stand mixer fitted with the beater, on medium speed for 3–5 minutes, until pale and creamy. Gradually, beat in the eggs, then the reserved orange zest. Sift the flour and ground ginger into a separate bowl, add the stem ginger and toss to coat each piece in the flour. Fold the flour mixture into the egg mixture until combined.

4 Divide the mixture equally between the pudding basins. Cover the puddings with the baking paper and foil circles (foil on top), securing them with string. Place the puddings in a roasting tin and pour in enough boiling water to come 2cm up the sides of the moulds. Bake for 40–45 minutes, until a skewer comes out clean.

5 **Make the crème anglaise.** Heat the milk, cream and vanilla seeds in a pan on a medium heat to just below boiling. In a bowl, whisk the egg yolks and sugar until pale and creamy. Pour in the warmed milk, whisking continuously, then return the mixture to the pan. Stir continuously over a very low heat for 3–4 minutes, until thick enough to coat the back of a spoon. Set aside.

6 To serve, warm the reserved orange and ginger syrups together. Turn out the puddings onto serving plates and drizzle them with the warmed syrup. Cut each orange spiral in half and arrange each pair on top of the pudding. Serve with the crème anglaise.

Apricot curd meringue roulade

Serves: 8
Hands on: 2 hours + chilling
Bake: 25 mins

FOR THE APRICOT CURD
250g apricots, halved and pitted
juice and finely grated zest of
 ½ unwaxed lemon
1 tsp vanilla paste
75g caster sugar
1 egg
1 egg yolk
25g unsalted butter

FOR THE MERINGUE ROULADE
6 egg whites
pinch of salt
300g caster sugar
1 tsp cornflour
1 tsp white wine vinegar
2 tsp vanilla paste

FOR THE CREAM FILLING
400ml double cream
1 tbsp icing sugar, sifted,
 plus extra for dusting
1 tsp vanilla paste

TO FILL AND DECORATE
4 apricots, halved, pitted and
 each half cut into 4 wedges
50g white chocolate, chopped
1 tbsp finely chopped pistachios
edible flowers (optional)

You will need
40 x 30cm Swiss roll or baking
 tin, about 4cm deep, greased,
 then lined (base and sides)
 with baking paper
large piping bag fitted with
 a medium star nozzle

A roulade is so much easier to make than it looks, but it never fails to impress as a summer centrepiece dessert. In this version, the tangy, smooth apricot curd filling delicately balances the sweetness and crispness of the meringue.

. . . .

1 **Make the apricot curd.** Cook the apricots with the lemon juice and zest, vanilla, half of the sugar and 1 tablespoon of water in a pan on a low heat, stirring until the sugar dissolves. Part-cover the pan with a lid and cook for 15 minutes, until the apricots break down. Press them through a fine-mesh sieve into a bowl to purée and return the purée to the pan.

2 Whisk together the egg, yolk and the remaining sugar. Add this to the apricot purée with the butter. Cook on a low heat, whisking continuously, for 1–2 minutes, until the mixture thickly coats the back of a spoon. Spoon into a clean bowl, cover the surface and leave to cool. Chill for 2 hours, or until needed.

3 **Make the meringue.** Heat the oven to 180°C/160°C fan/Gas 4. Whisk the egg whites and salt in a stand mixer fitted with the whisk on medium speed until the whites hold a soft peak. Slowly add the sugar, whisking continuously until the meringue is smooth and firm. In a bowl, combine the cornflour, vinegar and vanilla. Add this to the meringue and mix on low for 30 seconds.

4 Spoon the meringue into the prepared tin and spread it evenly using a palette knife. Bake for 15 minutes. Reduce the oven to 170°C/150°C fan/Gas 3. Turn the tray around to ensure the meringue cooks evenly and bake for a further 10 minutes, until the top is pale golden and crisp. Leave to cool in the tin.

5 **Make the cream filling.** In a bowl, whisk the cream, icing sugar and vanilla to soft peaks.

6 **Assemble the roulade.** Turn the cooled meringue out of the tin onto a large, clean sheet of baking paper and peel off the lining. Spread two-thirds of the cream filling over the meringue, scatter with half the apricots and spoon the apricot curd on top in an even layer. Starting at one of the shorter ends, roll the meringue into a neat roulade, then carefully slide it onto a serving plate seam-side down. Cover and chill for 30 minutes to firm up; and cover and chill the remaining cream filling.

7 To serve, melt the white chocolate in a bowl set over a pan of gently simmering water. Stir until smooth, then cool slightly. Using a teaspoon, drizzle the white chocolate over the roulade. Spoon the remaining cream into the piping bag and pipe the cream on the top of the roulade. Decorate with the pistachios, remaining apricots, and flowers (if using). Dust with icing sugar.

Summer fruit crumble

Serves: 6
Hands on: 20 mins
Bake: 30 mins

FOR THE CRUMBLE TOPPING
175g self-raising flour
85g unsalted butter,
    cubed and chilled
45g demerara sugar
45g golden caster sugar
35g porridge oats
85g pecans, roughly chopped

FOR THE FILLING
500g rhubarb, cut into 2–3cm chunks
100g caster sugar
500g cooking apples, peeled, cored
    and cut into 2–3cm chunks
500g mixed berries, such as
    strawberries, halved or quartered,
    and raspberries (blackberries and
    gooseberries are also good)
1 tbsp cornflour
custard, ice cream or double cream,
    to serve

You will need
30 x 23cm baking dish, about
    5–6cm deep, or individual dishes

This fruit crumble is a firm family favourite. I bake it throughout the summer, using a variety of fruits fresh from my kitchen garden. Pecans provide a crunchy addition to the buttery crumble topping. There is simply no beating it!

1 **Make the crumble topping.** Put the flour in a large bowl and rub in the butter using your fingertips until the mixture resembles breadcrumbs and there are only very small pieces of butter remaining. Add both types of sugar, the porridge oats and the pecans and mix to combine.

2 Heat the oven to 190°C/170°C fan/Gas 5.

3 **Make the filling.** Put the rhubarb in a large, wide pan, add half of the caster sugar and 2 tablespoons of water. Cook on a medium heat for 5 minutes, until slightly softened, then add the apples and the remaining sugar. Stir to combine, half cover the pan with the lid and simmer for a further few minutes until the apples start to soften. Mix in the berries and cook for 2 minutes, until slightly softened.

4 **Assemble the crumble.** Remove the pan from the heat and, using a slotted spoon, transfer the fruit to the baking dish (or small dishes if you're making individual crumbles). Add the cornflour to the fruit liquid in the pan and mix it in to form a paste. Pour this into the dish with the fruit and mix lightly to combine.

5 Spoon the crumble topping evenly over the fruit, place the dish on a baking tray and bake the crumble for 25–30 minutes, until the topping is golden, and the fruit juices start to bubble around the edge. (Alternatively, if you're making individual crumbles, bake them for just 15–20 minutes.) Serve the crumble warm with custard, ice cream or double cream.

St Clement's trifle

This trifle is made in a square tin and served in neat slices for a modern take on a humble and much-loved dessert (with sugar sprinkles, too). If blood oranges are in season, use half blood orange/half regular orange juice for the jelly layer.

· · · · · · · · · · · ·

Serves: 10–12
Hands on: 2 hours
   + chilling and overnight setting
Bake: 25 mins

FOR THE SPONGE
125g unsalted butter,
   cubed and softened
125g golden caster sugar
2 eggs, lightly beaten
1 tsp vanilla paste
finely grated zest of
   ½ unwaxed lemon
finely grated zest of
   ½ small unwaxed orange
100g plain flour
1 tsp baking powder
50g ground almonds
pinch of salt
2 tbsp soured cream

FOR THE SYRUP
50g caster sugar
juice of ½ lemon
juice of ½ small orange
2 tbsp sherry

FOR THE JELLY
5 platinum-grade gelatine leaves
350ml freshly squeezed orange juice
   (use half regular oranges and half
   blood oranges if in season)
150ml freshly squeezed lemon juice
75g caster sugar
2 x 398g tins mandarin segments
   in juice, drained

FOR THE CUSTARD
2 platinum-grade gelatine leaves
400ml whole milk
75g caster sugar
1½ tbsp cornflour
3 egg yolks
1 tsp vanilla paste

FOR THE TOPPING
300ml double cream
1 tbsp hundreds and thousands
   or toasted flaked almonds

You will need
20cm loose-bottomed square cake tin,
   about 6cm deep, greased, then lined
   (base and sides) with baking paper

1 **Make the sponge.** Heat the oven to 180°C/160°C fan/Gas 4. Beat the butter and sugar in a stand mixer fitted with the beater, on medium speed for 3–4 minutes, scraping down the inside of the bowl from time to time, until pale and creamy. A little at a time, add the eggs, mixing well between each addition. Mix in the vanilla, and the lemon and orange zests until combined.

2 Sift the flour, baking powder, ground almonds and salt into the bowl and beat on low speed for another 20–30 seconds to thoroughly combine. Mix in the soured cream until combined. Spoon the mixture into the prepared tin and spread it level with a palette knife.

3 Bake the sponge on the middle shelf for 22–25 minutes, until risen and golden, and a skewer inserted into the centre comes out clean. Leave the sponge to cool in the tin for 2 minutes, then turn it out onto a wire rack to cool completely.

4 Wash and re-line the base and sides of the cake tin with a sheet of clean baking paper, making sure that the paper reaches the rim of the tin. Return the cooled cake to the tin.

5 **Make the syrup.** Heat the sugar, and lemon and orange juices in a small pan on a low heat, stirring occasionally to dissolve the sugar. Bring the juices to the boil and cook until reduced by half and syrupy. Pour the syrup into a small bowl, add the sherry and leave to cool. There is no need to wash the pan as you can use it again for the jelly. Brush the top of the sponge with half of the syrup and chill the sponge while you prepare the jelly layer. Save the rest of the syrup for later.

6 **Make the jelly.** Soak the 5 gelatine leaves in a bowl of cold water for 5 minutes, until soft and floppy. Heat half of the mixed citrus juices with the sugar in the pan on a medium heat, stirring to dissolve the sugar, then as soon as the juice is hot but not boiling, remove the pan from the heat.

7 Drain the gelatine leaves and shake off any excess water. Add the gelatine to the hot juice and whisk to combine. Pour the hot juice into the remaining citrus juice in a jug, whisk to combine and leave to cool to room temperature. Once the jelly is cold, chill it for 15 minutes, until thickened and just starting to set.

Continues overleaf

St Clement's trifle
continued

8 Meanwhile, pat dry the mandarin segments on kitchen paper and arrange these on top of the sponge. Pour the jelly over the segments and sponge in an even layer, then chill the part-assembled trifle for 1 hour, until set.

9 **Make the custard layer.** While the jelly is setting, soak the 2 gelatine leaves in a bowl of cold water for 5 minutes, until soft and floppy. Heat the milk in a pan on a medium heat until almost to the boil. Using a balloon whisk, whisk the sugar, cornflour, egg yolks and vanilla in a bowl until smooth. Add half of the hot milk to the egg-yolk mixture, whisking continuously until smooth. Return the mixture to the pan and cook on a low–medium heat until it comes to the boil. Simmer for 10–20 seconds, until the custard has thickened and there is no cornflour taste remaining. Drain the gelatine leaves, squeeze out any excess water, and whisk into the custard until melted and thoroughly combined.

10 Strain the custard into a clean bowl, cover the surface with a disc of baking paper and leave it to cool. Once it's cool, pour it over the set jelly layer, cover the tin and return the trifle to the fridge for another 2 hours, or overnight, until set.

11 **Make the topping.** Whisk the cream with the reserved syrup until soft peaks. Spread the cream over the top of the trifle and chill again for 1 hour. Lift the trifle out of the tin, using the baking paper and loose-bottomed tin to help you, then scatter over the hundreds and thousands or flaked almonds. Cut it into 10–12 neat slices, to serve.

Salted caramel praline soufflés with hot chocolate sauce

Makes: 6
Hands on: 1 hour + chilling
Bake: 20 mins

FOR THE PRALINE
100g caster sugar
75g flaked almonds
pinch of salt

FOR THE SOUFFLÉS
3 large eggs, separated,
    plus 1 extra white
75g caster sugar
75g plain flour
1 tsp vanilla paste
300ml whole milk
pinch of salt
pinch of cream of tartar
icing sugar, for dusting

FOR THE CHOCOLATE SAUCE
40g caster sugar
250ml double cream
pinch of sea-salt flakes
125g 70% dark chocolate, chopped

You will need
baking tray, lined with a
    silicone mat or baking paper
150ml straight-sided ramekins x 6,
    brushed with melted butter and
    dusted with caster sugar

These pots of deliciousness are sure to help you let go of any soufflé insecurities. You can prepare them almost entirely in advance, with just a final flourish on the day.

. . . .

1 **Make the praline.** Heat the sugar with 1 tablespoon of water in a non-stick frying pan on a low heat until the sugar dissolves. Brush the sides of the pan with hot water to dislodge any sugar crystals. Bring the liquid to the boil over a medium heat and cook, swirling the pan occasionally, until you have an amber caramel. Stir in the flaked almonds and salt and cook for a further 15 seconds. Pour the praline evenly into the lined baking tray and leave it to cool and harden. Once it's hard, break up the praline and then whizz it in a food processor to finely chop. Set aside.

2 **Make the soufflés.** Whisk the egg yolks, sugar, flour and vanilla in a large bowl using a balloon whisk. Heat the milk in a pan on a medium heat until almost boiling, then pour it over the egg-yolk mixture, whisking continuously until smooth. Return the mixture to the pan and cook on a low heat, whisking continuously, until thickened to the consistency of lemon curd. Pour the mixture into a large bowl, cover the surface with a disc of baking paper and leave to cool. Chill until ready to use.

3 Heat the oven to 190°C/170°C fan/Gas 5. Beat the soufflé mixture until smooth and mix in 100g of the praline (save any leftover praline in an airtight jar for sprinkling over ice cream).

4 Whisk the reserved egg whites, plus the extra white, salt and cream of tartar in a stand mixer to stiff but not dry peaks. Fold one-third of the egg whites into the soufflé mixture using a large metal spoon. Fold in the remaining whites, taking care not to deflate the mixture. Spoon the soufflé mixture into the prepared ramekins so that it mounds up in the middle. Using a palette knife, quickly slice off the mound so the soufflé is level with the top of the ramekin and has a smooth, flat surface. Run a thumb around the inside top edge and arrange the ramekins on a baking tray. Bake for 20 minutes, until risen and golden.

5 **Make the chocolate sauce.** While the soufflés are baking, heat the sugar and 1½ teaspoons of water in a small pan on a low heat, without stirring, until the sugar dissolves. Bring to the boil and cook the syrup until you have an amber caramel. Slide the pan off the heat, slowly stir in the cream and add the sea salt, then return to a low heat to melt any hardened caramel. When smooth, add the chocolate and remove the pan from the heat. Stir gently until smooth. Dust the soufflés with icing sugar and serve them immediately with the warm chocolate sauce.

Panna cotta tart with berry jelly

A winning combination of jelly and (posh) custard in a buttery pastry case, this is a custard tart of dreams.

. . . .

Serves: 8
Hands on: 2 hours + chilling
Bake time: 30 mins

FOR THE PASTRY
225g plain flour
pinch of salt
125g unsalted butter,
    cubed and chilled
50g icing sugar, sifted
1 egg yolk
2 tbsp ice-cold water
2 tsp lemon juice

FOR THE PANNA COTTA
600ml double cream,
    plus 150ml to serve
75g caster sugar
½ vanilla pod, seeds scraped out
3 strips of unwaxed lemon peel
3 strips of unwaxed orange peel
3 platinum-grade gelatine leaves
300ml full-fat crème fraîche

FOR THE JELLY
250g raspberries,
    plus extra to decorate
250g redcurrants,
    plus extra to decorate
100g caster sugar
juice of ½ lemon
1½ platinum-grade
    gelatine leaves

You will need
23cm loose-bottomed
    fluted tart tin
heavy baking sheet
baking beans
small piping bag fitted with
    a medium open star nozzle

1 **Make the pastry case.** Tip the flour and salt into a large bowl. Using your fingertips, rub in the butter until the mixture resembles breadcrumbs. Using a table knife, mix in the icing sugar, then the egg yolk, water and lemon juice. Use your hands to gather the pastry into a ball and flatten it into a disc, then wrap and chill it for 1 hour, until firm.

2 Lightly flour the work surface and roll out the dough into a neat disc, about 2–3mm thick. Use this to line the base and sides of the tin, trimming any excess pastry, and chill for 20 minutes.

3 Meanwhile, heat the oven to 180°C/160°C fan/Gas 4 and place the baking sheet on the middle shelf. Prick the base of the pastry case, line it with baking paper and fill it with baking beans. Bake the case on top of the hot baking sheet for 20 minutes, until pale golden. Remove the lining and beans and bake for a further 10 minutes to cook the base. Leave to cool.

4 **Make the panna cotta.** Put the cream, sugar, vanilla seeds, scraped pod and strips of lemon and orange peel in a pan. Bring slowly to just below the boil, stirring occasionally. Remove from the heat and leave to infuse for 30 minutes. Soak the gelatine leaves in a bowl of cold water for 5 minutes, until softened.

5 Return the infused cream to a low heat and bring to just below the boil. Remove from the heat, drain the gelatine, squeeze out the excess water and whisk into the hot cream. Whisk in the crème fraîche until smooth. Strain the mixture into the pastry case and leave to cool, then chill for 2–3 hours, until set.

6 **Make the jelly.** Meanwhile, tip the fruit into a pan, add the sugar and lemon juice and cook on a low heat for 10 minutes, stirring often, until very soft and juicy. Strain into a bowl, leaving the juice to drip through for 1 hour without pressing the fruit (to keep the jelly clear). Measure 250ml of the juice, adding a little water if needed. Discard the remainder and the pulp.

7 Soak the 1½ gelatine leaves in a bowl of cold water for 5 minutes to soften. Heat 3 tablespoons of the berry juice to just boiling. Add the drained gelatine leaves to the hot juice and stir until melted. Stir the jelly mixture into the reserved juice, then carefully pour it over the top of the panna cotta and return the dessert to the fridge for a further 1–2 hours, until set.

8 Whip the extra 150ml of cream to soft peaks. Spoon this into the piping bag and pipe around the edge of the tart. Decorate with berries to serve.

Lemon meringue tarts

This 70s classic is given the modern patisserie treatment in individual tarts with beautifully piped Swiss meringue. They make for an elegant and sophisticated afternoon tea.

. . . .

Makes: 8
Hands on: 1½ hours + chilling
Bake: 25 mins

FOR THE PASTRY
100g unsalted butter,
    cubed and softened
50g icing sugar, sifted
2 egg yolks
175g plain flour
pinch of salt
1 tbsp whole milk

FOR THE LEMON CURD
150g caster sugar
juice and finely grated zest
    of 3 unwaxed lemons
4 egg yolks (save the whites
    for the meringue)
1 egg
2 tsp cornflour
pinch of salt
75g unsalted butter,
    cubed and softened

FOR THE SWISS MERINGUE
4 egg whites
250g caster sugar
pinch of salt

You will need
8cm diameter tart rings or
    tins x 8, set on a baking sheet
    lined with baking paper
baking beans
large piping bag fitted
    with a medium star
    or St Honoré nozzle
kitchen blow torch

1 **Make the pastry cases.** Beat the butter and icing sugar in a stand mixer fitted with the beater, on medium speed for 2–3 minutes, until pale and creamy. Mix in the egg yolks. Scrape down the bowl and add the flour, salt and half the milk. Mix on low until the dough starts to clump together, adding the remaining milk, if needed. Tip out the dough onto the work surface and lightly knead it to bring it together into a smooth ball. Flatten the pastry into a disc, then wrap and chill it for at least 1 hour, until firm.

2 Flour the work surface, divide the pastry equally into eight and roll out each portion into a 12cm disc, about 2–3mm thick. On the lined baking sheet, line the base and the sides of each tart ring or case with the pastry. Trim any excess and chill for 30 minutes. Meanwhile, heat the oven to 180°C/160°C fan/Gas 4.

3 Prick the base of the chilled tart cases with a fork, line them with baking paper and baking beans and bake for 14 minutes, until pale golden. Remove the paper and beans and bake for a further 2 minutes to dry out and crisp the base. Leave to cool.

4 **Make the lemon curd.** While the pastry cases are cooling, tip half of the sugar into a pan and add the lemon juice. Tip the remaining sugar into a large heatproof bowl and whisk with the egg yolks, egg, cornflour and salt until combined. Heat the lemon juice and sugar over a low–medium heat, stirring to dissolve the sugar and bring to just below boiling. Pour the hot juice onto the egg mixture, whisking continuously until smooth. Pour it back into the pan and cook the curd over a low heat for 2 minutes, whisking until thickened to a pouring custard consistency.

5 Spoon the curd into a bowl and whisk with the lemon zest and butter until combined. Divide the curd between the pastry cases, spreading it level. Bake for 8–10 minutes, until set. Leave to cool.

6 **Make the Swiss meringue.** Combine the egg whites, sugar, salt and 1 tablespoon of water in a heatproof bowl set over a pan of gently simmering water and mix with a balloon whisk for 3–4 minutes, until the sugar dissolves, and the mixture is hot to the touch and thick enough to leave a loose ribbon trail when you lift the whisk. Transfer the meringue to a stand mixer fitted with a whisk and whisk for 2–3 minutes, until stiff and glossy.

7 **Finish the tarts.** Spoon the meringue into the piping bag and pipe it over the top of each tart. Scorch the top of the meringue using the blow torch and leave to cool before serving.

Sticky toffee chocolate puddings

Makes: 10
Hands on: 30 mins
Bake: 25 mins

FOR THE PUDDINGS
100g blanched hazelnuts
100g milk chocolate, chopped
100g unsalted butter,
    cubed and softened
175g light muscovado sugar
2 large eggs, lightly beaten
225g self-raising flour
½ tsp baking powder
½ tsp bicarbonate of soda
275ml whole milk,
    at room temperature

FOR THE SAUCE
100g unsalted butter, cubed
125g light muscovado sugar
1 tbsp black treacle
250ml double cream
1 tsp vanilla extract
75g milk chocolate,
    finely chopped

You will need
150ml pudding basins x 10,
    greased, then base-lined
    with a disc of baking paper

These puddings are a firm family favourite in my household. I usually make them on a Sunday to serve after our roast dinner. The kids absolutely love them and there are always plenty to go round for second helpings, too!

1 **Roast the hazelnuts.** Heat the oven to 180°C/160°C fan/Gas 4. Place the hazelnuts on a baking tray and toast them in the oven for 5 minutes, until golden. Roughly chop half of the hazelnuts, leaving some whole. Reduce the oven temperature to 170°C/150°C fan/Gas 3.

2 **Make the puddings.** Melt the chocolate in a heatproof bowl set over a pan of gently simmering water or in a microwave. Stir the chocolate until melted and smooth, then leave to cool slightly.

3 Meanwhile, beat the butter and sugar in a stand mixer fitted with the beater, on medium speed for 3–4 minutes, scraping down the inside of the bowl from time to time, until pale and creamy. A little at a time, add the eggs, mixing well between each addition. Stir in the melted chocolate.

4 Sift the flour, baking powder and bicarbonate of soda into the bowl. Divide the hazelnuts into two equal portions. Little by little, fold one portion into the pudding mixture, alternating with the milk.

5 Divide the mixture equally between the prepared pudding moulds. Bake the puddings for 25 minutes, until they are risen and springy to the touch, and a skewer inserted into the centres comes out clean.

6 **Make the sauce.** While the puddings are baking, heat all the ingredients for the sauce in a pan on a low–medium heat, stirring continuously to melt the butter and dissolve the sugar. Simmer the sauce, stirring continuously for 1 minute, until thickened.

7 Once the puddings are ready, use a palette knife to release them from the moulds, then carefully turn them out onto serving plates. Pour the sauce over and scatter with the reserved portion of hazelnuts. Serve warm.

Rhubarb crumble pots

Serves: 6
Hands on: 45 mins + chilling
Bake: 15 mins

FOR THE BAKED RHUBARB
500g forced pink rhubarb,
    cut into 3cm-long pieces
50g caster sugar
juice of 1 orange, preferably
    blood orange
½ vanilla pod, split lengthways

FOR THE CRUMBLE
75g unsalted butter
75g light muscovado sugar
110g white rye, spelt or plain flour
½ tsp ground cinnamon
½ tsp ground cardamom
pinch of salt
40g flaked almonds

FOR THE CUSTARD
500ml whole milk
½ vanilla pod, split lengthways
2 strips of unwaxed orange zest
4 egg yolks
100g caster sugar
2 tbsp cornflour

You will need
baking tray, lined with baking paper

Rhubarb crumble and custard must be a favourite Sunday lunch pudding up and down the land. Here, it is given an elegant spin and served chilled and deconstructed with a nutty, spiced crumble, in individual portions.

· · · · · · · · · · · · ·

1 **Start the baked rhubarb.** Tip the rhubarb into a roasting tin or ovenproof dish, sprinkle with the sugar and set aside for 10 minutes. Meanwhile, heat the oven to 190°C/170°C fan/Gas 5.

2 **Make the crumble.** Melt the butter in a small pan or microwave. Pour the melted butter into a large bowl and leave it to cool slightly. Mix in the muscovado sugar, flour, spices and salt to combine. Tip the mixture into the lined baking tray, spread it out evenly and bake it for 15 minutes, stirring every 5 minutes to break up the crumble, until crisp. Add the flaked almonds and cook for a further 1 minute, until golden. Leave to cool.

3 **Bake the rhubarb.** While the crumble is baking, add the orange juice and halved vanilla pod to the rhubarb. Cover the tin or dish loosely with foil and bake the fruit for 15 minutes, until it's tender but still holds its shape. Leave to cool.

4 **Make the custard.** Pour the milk into a small pan, then add the vanilla pod and strips of orange zest. Place the pan on a low heat and bring the milk to a simmer, then remove the pan from the heat and leave the milk to infuse for 15 minutes.

5 In a large bowl, whisk the egg yolks, sugar and cornflour until smooth and combined. Reheat the milk to just below boiling and pour it into the bowl, whisking continuously until smooth. Return the mixture to the pan and cook on a low–medium heat, whisking continuously, until the custard starts to bubble, thickly coats the back of a spoon and the cornflour has been cooked out. Strain the custard into a clean bowl, cover the surface with a disc of baking paper and leave it to cool for 15 minutes.

6 **Assemble the pots.** Divide the custard between six glasses or individual serving dishes, cover and chill for 30 minutes, until set. Spoon the rhubarb on top of the custard and scatter with the crumble just before serving.

7
Chocolate

Double-trouble chocolate cake

Serves: 10–12
Hands on: 2 hours + chilling
Bake: 25 mins

FOR THE SPONGES
175g 70% dark chocolate, chopped
175g unsalted butter, cubed
125ml hot strong coffee
3 eggs
125ml buttermilk,
    at room temperature
2 tbsp sunflower oil
1 tsp vanilla paste
150g golden caster sugar
150g light brown soft sugar
260g plain flour
40g cocoa powder
1½ tsp bicarbonate of soda
½ tsp baking powder
pinch of salt

FOR THE FUDGE FROSTING
175g 70% dark chocolate, chopped
200g unsalted butter,
    cubed and softened
125g icing sugar, sifted
100g condensed milk
1 tsp vanilla paste
pinch of salt

FOR THE CHOCOLATE SWISS MERINGUE BUTTERCREAM
200g 70% dark chocolate, chopped
175g caster sugar
3 egg whites
pinch of salt
250g unsalted butter, cubed
    and softened

You will need
20cm round cake tins x 3, greased,
    then base-lined with baking paper
2 piping bags, each fitted with
    a medium plain nozzle

Silky chocolate buttercream and dark fudge frosting earn their stripes in this decadent chocolate extravaganza, which is laced with just a hint of coffee for extra richness.

. . . .

1 **Make the sponges.** Heat the oven to 180°C/160°C fan/Gas 4. Melt the chocolate and butter with the coffee in a heatproof bowl set over a pan of gently simmering water and whisk to combine. Remove the bowl from the heat and leave to cool slightly.

2 In a large bowl, use a balloon whisk to beat the eggs, buttermilk, sunflower oil and vanilla until combined. Whisk in both types of sugar, then the melted chocolate mixture until smooth. Sift the flour, cocoa powder, bicarbonate of soda, baking powder and salt into the bowl and whisk until combined. Divide the mixture equally between the prepared tins and bake for 25 minutes, until a skewer inserted into the centres comes out clean. Leave the sponges to cool in the tins for 10 minutes, then carefully turn them out onto a wire rack to cool completely.

3 **Make the fudge frosting.** Melt the chocolate in a bowl over a pan of gently simmering water. Stir, remove from the heat and leave to cool slightly. Beat the butter and icing sugar in a stand mixer on medium speed for 3–5 minutes, until pale and creamy. Mix in the condensed milk, vanilla and salt. Lower the speed and briefly mix in the melted chocolate. Cover and set aside.

4 **Make the chocolate buttercream.** Melt the chocolate as in Step 3. Put the sugar, egg whites, salt and 1 tablespoon of water in a clean heatproof bowl set over the pan of simmering water. Whisk until the sugar dissolves. Cook for another 3 minutes, whisking continuously, until the mixture thickens enough to hold a ribbon trail. Spoon the mixture into a stand mixer and whisk on medium–high for 3 minutes, until doubled in volume and cold. Gradually add the butter, beating continuously until smooth. Fold in the melted chocolate, cover and set aside.

5 **Assemble the cake.** Spoon half the buttercream into one piping bag with a medium plain nozzle and half the fudge frosting into the other. Place one sponge on a serving plate, level the top if domed and pipe a ring of buttercream around the top edge. Pipe a ring of fudge frosting inside the buttercream, then pipe alternate rings to cover the cake. Top with the second sponge and repeat the piping. Place the third sponge on top and gently press down.

6 Refill the bags with the remaining frosting and buttercream. Pipe rings of the chocolate frosting up the side of the cake, then smooth it over using a palette knife, pressing the edge of the knife into the frosting to give texture. Pipe kisses of both fillings over the top of the cake. Chill for 30 minutes to 1 hour before serving.

Prue's caramelised white chocolate & blackcurrant cheesecakes

Baking white chocolate in a low oven caramelises the sugars to create 'blonde' chocolate, which has a distinctive, nutty sweetness. This, in turn, brings a whole new level of flavour to these cheesecakes.

Makes: 6
Hands on: 1 hour 20 mins + chilling
Bake: 40 mins

FOR THE BISCUIT BASE
30g plain flour
pinch of salt
30g porridge oats
30g caster sugar
50g unsalted butter
35g runny honey

FOR THE BLACKCURRANT JELLY
2½ platinum-grade gelatine leaves
150g blackcurrants, fresh, or frozen and defrosted
50g caster sugar

FOR THE CARAMELISED WHITE CHOCOLATE
170g white chocolate, chopped

FOR THE FILLING
135g full-fat cream cheese
1 egg
1 egg yolk
1 tsp cornflour, sifted
100ml double cream

FOR THE CHOCOLATE DECORATION
100g white chocolate, chopped

TO DECORATE
125ml double cream
¼ tsp vanilla extract
2 tsp icing sugar, sifted
6 blackcurrants and blackcurrant leaves (optional)

Continues overleaf

1 **Make the biscuit base.** Heat the oven to 190°C/170°C fan/ Gas 5. Tip the flour, salt, oats and caster sugar into a large bowl. Using your fingertips, rub 15g of the butter into the flour mixture until it resembles breadcrumbs. Stir in the honey, then sprinkle the crumb mixture evenly over the lined baking tray and bake for 8–10 minutes, until golden. Remove from the oven and leave the biscuit crumbs to cool on the tray. Turn the oven down to 170°C/150°C fan/Gas 3.

2 **Make the blackcurrant jelly.** While the crumbs are baking, soak the gelatine leaves in a bowl of cold water for 5 minutes to soften. Place the blackcurrants in a mini food processor and blitz to a purée.

3 Pass the blackcurrant purée through a fine-mesh, nylon sieve into a small pan, then add the sugar and 3 tablespoons of water. Place the pan on a medium heat and bring the blackcurrant purée to the boil, then remove from the heat.

4 Drain the gelatine leaves, squeezing out any excess water, then add them to the hot purée. Stir to melt the gelatine, then pour the blackcurrant mixture into the silicone-lined tray in an even layer. Leave to cool, then chill for 30 minutes, until set.

5 **Finish the cheesecake base.** Blitz the cooled biscuit into fine crumbs in a food processor.

6 Melt the remaining 35g of butter in a small pan, remove the pan from the heat and stir in the biscuit crumbs until coated and combined. Divide the mixture equally between the 6 holes of the silicone mould or 6 chef's rings, pressing it down with the base of a glass or the end of a rolling pin to an even layer. Chill in the freezer for 10 minutes to firm up.

7 **Make the caramelised white chocolate.** Tip the white chocolate into a heatproof bowl and microwave it on high for 30 seconds, then stir it with a spatula. Repeat the 30 seconds in the microwave between 15 and 20 times, stirring after every 30 seconds, until the chocolate is golden brown in colour – take care as the bowl will get very hot; use oven gloves each time you remove it from the microwave to stir. During the process, the chocolate becomes lumpy and chalky, but keep stirring it until it's smooth again. Once it's ready, leave it to cool while you prepare the rest of the filling.

Continues overleaf

Prue's caramelised white chocolate & blackcurrant cheesecakes
continued

You will need
baking tray, lined
   with baking paper
15 x 10cm shallow tray,
   lined with a silicone mat
7cm x 6-hole silicone mould;
   or 7cm chef's rings x 6,
   lined with baking paper
cooking thermometer
sheet of acetate
7cm round cutter
small piping bag fitted
   with a small ribbon nozzle

8 **Make the filling.** Beat the cream cheese in a stand mixer fitted with the beater, on medium speed until smooth. Add the egg and egg yolk and continue to beat until smooth again. Add the caramelised chocolate, cornflour and cream, then beat on low speed until well mixed.

9 Pour equal amounts of the filling over each biscuit base and bake for 25–30 minutes, until the cheesecakes start to brown, but still have a slight wobble in the centre. Remove them from the oven, leave them to cool, then chill for 1 hour, until firm.

10 **Make the chocolate decoration.** First, temper the white chocolate by melting 75g of the white chocolate in a heatproof bowl set over a pan of gently simmering water. Heat it until it reaches 40°C on the cooking thermometer, stirring occasionally so it melts evenly. Remove the bowl from the pan and leave it to stand for 10 minutes, then stir in the remaining chocolate. Stir continuously until the chocolate cools to 25°C, then place the bowl back over the pan of simmering water and stir until the chocolate reaches 27°C.

11 Lay the sheet of acetate on your work surface and, using a palette knife, spread the tempered white chocolate on top in an even layer, about 3mm thick. Leave for 10 minutes, until almost set, then cut the chocolate into triangles of about 9 x 9 x 4cm. Leave the chocolate triangles to set completely, then carefully peel them off the acetate.

12 **Assemble the cheesecakes.** Once chilled, pop the cheesecakes out of the moulds and place each one on a serving plate. Using the 7cm round cutter, cut 6 rounds from the set blackcurrant jelly and place one on top of each cheesecake.

13 **Decorate the cheesecakes.** Whip the double cream, vanilla and icing sugar together to medium peaks, then spoon the sweetened cream into the small piping bag fitted with a small ribbon nozzle. Pipe a wavy line down the middle of each cheesecake, then position a white chocolate triangle at one end. Finish with blackcurrants and blackcurrant leaves, if using.

Double-cherry double-nut tiffin

Makes: 20
Hands on: 40 mins + chilling
Bake: 12 mins

FOR THE DIGESTIVE BISCUITS
60g plain wholemeal flour
60g plain flour
50g oat bran or medium oatmeal
¼ tsp bicarbonate of soda
¼ tsp ground cardamom
¼ tsp ground cinnamon
pinch of salt
100g unsalted butter,
   cubed and chilled
50g soft light brown sugar
1 tbsp whole milk

FOR THE TIFFIN
100g macadamia nuts
100g pecan nuts
150g dried sour cherries
75g glacé cherries, rinsed
   and patted dry, then halved
75g unsweetened desiccated coconut
200g 70% dark chocolate, chopped
150g milk chocolate, chopped
175g unsalted butter
175g golden syrup

FOR THE TOPPING
100g 70% dark chocolate, chopped
100g milk chocolate, chopped
15g unsalted butter
50g white chocolate,
   chopped and melted

You will need
large baking sheet,
   lined with baking paper
30 x 20cm baking tin,
   lined (base and sides)
   with baking paper
small piping bag fitted with
   a small writing nozzle
small wooden skewer
   or cocktail stick

Double deliciousness for this tiffin, with two types of nut and two types of cherry folded into a crumbly digestive base.

· · · · · · · · · · · · ·

1 **Make the biscuits.** Sift both flours, the oat bran or oatmeal, bicarbonate of soda, spices and salt into a large bowl, tipping in any bran left in the sieve. Add the butter and rub it in until you have a breadcrumb texture. Mix in the sugar. Pour in the milk and mix with a round-bladed knife until the dough starts to clump together. Then, knead it to a neat, smooth ball and flatten it into a disc. Wrap the dough and chill it for 1 hour, until firm.

2 Lightly dust the work surface with flour and roll out the dough into a square, about 3–4mm thick. Using a sharp knife, cut the dough into twenty 5cm squares and arrange these on the lined baking sheet, leaving space between each one. Chill the dough for 20 minutes while you heat the oven to 170°C/150°C fan/Gas 3.

3 Bake the biscuits on the middle shelf for 12 minutes, until firm and light golden. Remove them from the oven and leave to cool on the tray. Leave the oven on.

4 **Start the tiffin.** Tip both types of nut onto a baking tray and toast them in the oven for 4 minutes, until golden. Roughly chop and leave to cool. Break the cooled biscuits into 1–2cm pieces and tip them into a large bowl with the chopped nuts, both types of cherry and the coconut, then mix to combine.

5 Melt both chocolates in a large heatproof bowl set over a pan of gently simmering water, stir until smooth and remove from the heat. In a pan, melt the butter with the golden syrup, stir, then remove from the heat and leave to cool slightly.

6 Mix the butter and golden syrup mixture into the melted chocolate, then mix this into the biscuit mixture. Spoon into the prepared baking tin and press the mixture level. Cover the surface with a sheet of baking paper and press the surface flat using a flat-bottomed ramekin or glass. Chill for 1 hour, until firm.

7 **Make the topping.** Melt the dark and milk chocolates together with the butter in a heatproof bowl set over a pan of gently simmering water. Stir until smooth, then leave to cool slightly. Pour the chocolate over the top of the chilled tiffin and spread it level. Spoon the melted white chocolate into the piping bag fitted with a small writing nozzle. Pipe straight lines of chocolate, about 1 cm apart over the tiffin. Working perpendicular to the lines, drag the tip of the cocktail stick or skewer through the piped chocolate in alternate directions to give a feather effect.

8 Chill the tiffin for 30 minutes, until set, then cut it into equal-sized squares to serve.

BAKER'S RECIPE
Chocolate, hazelnut & almond dacquoise

Serves: 10
Hands on: 45 mins + chilling
Bake: 25 mins

**FOR THE CHOCOLATE
CRÉMEUX FILLING**
120ml whole milk
225ml whipping cream
6 egg yolks (save the whites
for the dacquoise)
45g caster sugar
285g 70% dark chocolate, chopped
30g unsalted butter,
cubed and softened

FOR THE DACQUOISE
175g ground hazelnuts
100g ground almonds
60g cornflour
375g caster sugar
6 large egg whites
pinch of salt
50g flaked almonds
icing sugar, sifted, for dusting

TO DECORATE
75g blanched hazelnuts
100g 70% dark chocolate,
roughly chopped
200ml double cream
icing sugar, sifted, for dusting

You will need
20cm cake tin or plate as a template
3 baking trays, each lined with
a sheet of baking paper
2 piping bags: one fitted with
a large plain nozzle and one
with a medium star nozzle
small piping bag fitted with
a small plain writing nozzle
small baking sheet, lined with
baking paper

This is my favourite cake to make for family gatherings, because it cheekily contains all my own favourite dessert ingredients! I always make sure I get the biggest slice – I think of it as baker's perks.

. . . .

1 **Make the crémeux filling.** Bring the milk and cream to the boil in a small pan. Whisk the egg yolks and sugar in a heatproof bowl with a balloon whisk for 2 minutes, until pale. Slowly pour the hot cream over the eggs, whisking continuously, then return the mixture to the pan. Cook on a low heat, without boiling, and stirring continuously, until the cream mixture thickens enough to coat the back of a spoon.

2 Tip the chocolate into a large heatproof bowl. Strain the hot cream mixture over the chocolate, leave for a minute, then gently mix with a rubber spatula to melt the chocolate. Add the butter, then stir until it melts and the crémeux is smooth. Cover the surface with a disc of baking paper to prevent a skin forming, leave to cool, then chill for 2 hours, until set.

3 **Make the roasted hazelnuts to decorate.** Heat the oven to 180°C/160°C fan/Gas 4. Spread the blanched hazelnuts onto a separate, unlined baking tray and roast them for 5 minutes, until light golden and toasted. Set aside and leave to cool. Leave the oven on.

4 **Make the dacquoise.** Using the 20cm cake tin or plate as a guide, draw a circle on each sheet of baking paper lining the three baking trays and turn the sheets drawn-side down.

5 In a bowl, combine the ground hazelnuts, ground almonds, cornflour and 125g of the caster sugar.

6 Whisk the egg whites with the salt in a stand mixer or using an electric hand whisk until you have firm, but not dry peaks. Gradually, whisk in the remaining sugar, until the meringue is smooth, thick and glossy, and holds a firm peak. Using a large metal spoon or rubber spatula, fold in the ground nut mixture, then spoon it into the piping bag fitted with a large plain nozzle.

7 Pipe a disc of the meringue onto each sheet of baking paper, using the drawn circles as a guide and working outwards from the middle of each circle. Clean the piping bag and nozzle.

8 Scatter the flaked almonds over the meringues and lightly dust them with icing sugar. Bake them for 20–25 minutes, until crisp on top and golden. Remove the baking trays from the oven and leave the meringues on them to cool.

Continues overleaf

Chocolate, hazelnut & almond dacquoise
continued

9 **Assemble the dacquoise.** Soften the crémeux for 10 seconds in the microwave or in a bowl of warm water if it is too firm to spread. Reserve 3 tablespoons of the crémeux and spoon the remainder into the cleaned piping bag fitted with a large plain nozzle. Place one of the meringue discs on a serving plate and pipe large blobs of crémeux over the surface. Cover with the second meringue and repeat with the remaining crémeux in the piping bag. Top with the third meringue disc, gently pressing the layers together.

10 **Make the chocolate decorations**. Melt the chocolate in a heatproof bowl set over a pan of gently simmering water. Spoon the melted chocolate into the small piping bag fitted with a small plain writing nozzle. Pipe 10–12 squiggly chocolate decorations onto the lined small baking sheet and transfer them to the fridge to set (about 30 minutes).

11 Whisk the double cream with the reserved 3 tablespoons of crémeux in a large bowl until it just holds a firm peak, then spoon it into the piping bag fitted with a medium star nozzle. Pipe rosettes around the edge of the top of the dacquoise and decorate with the chocolate decorations and roasted hazelnuts, evenly spacing them among the rosettes.

Gooey chocolate & caramel tart

If chocolate and sugar are your thing, this tart – filled with chocolate ganache with a caramel swirl – is going to hit the spot. The chocolate caramel ganache is an involved process, but remember: the best things come to those who wait!

. . . .

Serves: 8–10
Hands on: 1½ hours + chilling
Bake: 30 mins

FOR THE PASTRY
75g unsalted butter, cubed
50g icing sugar, sifted
1 egg, beaten
150g plain flour
1 tbsp cocoa powder
¼ tsp salt

FOR THE CARAMEL
120ml double cream
¼ tsp salt
½ vanilla pod, seeds scraped out
100g caster sugar
2 tsp golden syrup
30g cold unsalted butter, cubed

FOR THE CHOCOLATE-CARAMEL GANACHE
280g 70% dark chocolate, chopped
120ml double cream,
    at room temperature
85g unsalted butter
200g caster sugar
1 tbsp golden syrup
½ tsp salt
3 eggs
1 vanilla pod, seeds scraped out

TO DECORATE
150g 70% dark chocolate, chopped

You will need
23cm shallow (Continental),
    loose-bottomed fluted tart tin
baking beans
medium piping bag fitted
    with a medium plain nozzle
cooking thermometer
30 x 7cm strips of acetate x 3
baking sheet
chocolate comb or grouting tool
3 inner cardboard tubes
    from a kitchen roll

1 **Make the pastry.** Beat the butter and icing sugar in the bowl of a stand mixer fitted with the beater, on low–medium speed for 5 minutes, until smooth. Add the egg, increase the speed to medium and beat for 1 minute, until combined and smooth. Gradually add the flour, cocoa powder and salt on low speed, scraping down the inside of the bowl if needed. Mix until just combined, taking care not to overmix. Tip out the dough onto a lightly floured work surface and knead it to bring it together into a neat, smooth ball. Wrap it and chill it for at least 1 hour.

2 **Make the caramel.** Gently heat the cream, salt, vanilla pod and seeds in a small pan on a medium heat, stirring occasionally and without boiling. In a separate pan, mix the sugar, golden syrup and 2 tablespoons of water with your fingers until the mixture feels sandy. Heat on a low–medium heat until the sugar dissolves, then cook, swirling the pan occasionally, to a deep mahogany-brown syrup. Reduce the heat to low, then gradually whisk in the warm cream – the sugar will bubble up so take care. Remove the pan from the heat. A little at a time, whisk in the butter, until you have a smooth caramel. Pass the caramel through a fine-mesh sieve into a bowl, leave it to cool, then chill until set.

3 **Make the pastry case.** Lightly flour the work surface and roll out the pastry to a 30cm circle, about 3mm thick. Using a rolling pin, carefully lift the pastry into the tart tin, then gently press it into the base and up the sides, taking care not to stretch it so that you avoid shrinkage during baking. Trim the excess pastry with a sharp knife, prick the base with a fork and chill the pastry case for 20 minutes. Heat the oven to 190°C/170°C fan/Gas 5.

4 Line the pastry case with baking paper and fill it with baking beans. Bake it for 20 minutes, until the top edge turns golden. Remove the beans and paper, then return the case to the oven for a further 5–10 minutes, until the base is dry. Leave to cool.

5 **Make the chocolate-caramel ganache.** While the pastry case is baking, melt the chocolate in a heatproof bowl set over a pan of gently simmering water. Stir, then remove the bowl from the pan and leave the chocolate to cool slightly.

6 In a small pan, heat the cream and butter until the butter melts, then remove the pan from the heat. Set aside.

Continues overleaf

Gooey chocolate & caramel tart
continued

7 In a separate pan, mix the sugar, golden syrup, salt and 2 tablespoons of water with your fingers until the mixture feels sandy. Heat over a low–medium heat until the sugar dissolves, then cook, swirling the pan occasionally, until you have a deep mahogany-brown syrup. Remove the pan from the heat and carefully pour in the warm cream mixture to make a caramel – take care as it will splutter. Set aside.

8 Whisk the eggs and vanilla seeds in a stand mixer fitted with a whisk, on medium speed until light and foamy, and the eggs hold a ribbon trail when you lift the whisk.

9 With the mixer on low speed, slowly drizzle the warm caramel into the egg foam. Increase the speed to medium and whisk for 5 minutes, until the mixture cools to room temperature. Reduce the speed of the mixer again and slowly add the warm melted chocolate and mix until it's just combined.

10 **Assemble the tart.** Spread a quarter of the chilled caramel over the base of the cooled tart case. Then, pour the chocolate ganache over the top and leave it to settle for 2–3 minutes, then level it with a palette knife.

11 Spoon the remaining caramel into the medium piping bag fitted with a plain nozzle. Pipe the caramel in an open spiral over the top of the tart, leaving space so the chocolate ganache shows through. The caramel will settle slightly into the chocolate, but you want to see both mixtures. Leave the tart to stand at room temperature for 30 minutes, then chill.

12 **Make the decorations.** First, temper the chocolate by melting 100g of the chocolate in a heatproof bowl set over a pan of gently simmering water, stirring continuously with a rubber spatula until it reaches 45°C on the cooking thermometer. Remove the bowl from the heat and add the remaining 50g of chocolate, stirring slowly and continuously until the chocolate cools to 28°C. Set the bowl back over the pan of gently simmering water and reheat the chocolate, stirring continuously until it reaches 31°C. Remove the bowl from the heat and leave the chocolate to cool slightly.

13 Lay the strips of acetate over the base of a damp baking sheet (the damp surface will prevent the acetate moving around). Spread the tempered chocolate over the acetate strips to cover. Comb the chocolate lengthways with a chocolate comb or grouting tool to create long strips. Curl the acetate strips into a loose spiral and place each one inside a cardboard tube until the chocolate sets.

14 Once set, peel the chocolate twists from the acetate and place them in the centre of the tart to decorate.

Chocolate & peanut brookies

Double chocolate brownies, with a satisfying dose of chocolate chips pressed into the surface, meet gooey white chocolate and peanut cookies to create these totally irresistible, where-have-you-been-all-my-life 'brookies'.

Makes: 12–16
Hands on: 40 mins
Bake: 30 mins

FOR THE COOKIE DOUGH
75g unsalted butter, softened
50g peanut butter
50g caster sugar
50g light brown soft sugar
1 tsp vanilla extract
1 egg, lightly beaten
150g plain flour
½ tsp baking powder
75g white chocolate,
    roughly chopped
50g salted peanuts,
    roughly chopped

FOR THE BROWNIE MIXTURE
125g 70% dark chocolate, chopped
125g 54% dark chocolate, chopped
150g unsalted butter, diced
3 eggs
125g light brown soft sugar
100g caster sugar
1 tsp vanilla extract
125g plain flour
½ tsp baking powder

TO FINISH
75g 70% dark chocolate, chopped
pinch of sea-salt flakes

You will need
30 x 20cm brownie tin, greased,
    then lined (base and sides)
    with baking paper

1 **Make the cookie dough.** Heat the oven to 180°C/160°C fan/Gas 4. Beat the butter, peanut butter, both types of sugar and the vanilla in a stand mixer fitted with the beater, on medium speed for 3 minutes, until pale and creamy. Scrape down the inside of the bowl, add the egg and mix again to combine. Sift in the flour and baking powder and mix on low speed for 20 seconds, until just combined. Stir in the white chocolate and peanuts, then spoon the mixture into a separate bowl and set aside.

2 **Make the brownie mixture.** Melt both dark chocolates and the butter in a heatproof bowl set over a pan of gently simmering water, stirring occasionally. Remove the bowl from the heat and leave the chocolate to cool for 3–4 minutes.

3 Meanwhile, whisk the eggs, both types of sugar and the vanilla in a stand mixer fitted with the whisk, on medium speed for 3 minutes, until pale and thickened. Stir in the melted chocolate until just combined. Sift in the flour and baking powder and fold in until smooth.

4 **Assemble the brookie.** Using a teaspoon, randomly drop dollops of one half of the cookie dough mixture into the prepared brownie tin. Pour the brownie mixture on top of the spoonfuls and spread it level.

5 Spoon dollops of the remaining cookie dough mixture randomly over the top and finish with a scattering of chopped dark chocolate and sea-salt flakes.

6 **Bake the brookie.** Place the tin on the middle shelf and bake the brookie for 25–30 minutes, until just set, and the top has lightly risen and started to crack. Leave to cool, then cut the brookie into 12–16 squares to serve.

Chocolate bread & butter pudding

Serves: 8
Hands on: 45 mins
  + infusing and chilling
Bake: 55 mins

FOR THE PUDDING
75g raisins
2 tbsp Madeira or brandy
250ml whole milk
250ml double cream
1 tsp ground cinnamon
½ vanilla pod, split in half
3 strips of unwaxed orange peel
275–300g small brioche buns,
    cut into 2cm pieces
50g unsalted butter, melted
125g 70% dark chocolate, chopped
3 eggs
3 yolks
100g golden caster sugar,
    plus 4 tbsp to serve
2 tbsp demerara sugar

FOR THE CUSTARD
225ml whole milk
125ml double cream
1 bay leaf
1 cinnamon stick
50g caster sugar
juice of 1 orange
3 egg yolks

You will need
20cm square baking tin or
    ovenproof dish, greased,
    then lined (base and sides)
    with baking paper
baking tray, lined with
    baking paper

Twice-baked, caramelised and served with burnt orange, bay and cinnamon custard, this is a truly sumptuous, indulgent and aromatic makeover for a cherished, traditional dessert.

· · · · · · · · · · · · · · ·

1 **Make the pudding.** Heat the raisins in the Madeira or brandy in a small pan on a low heat, until just about to boil. Tip it all into a bowl and leave to cool and plump up. Pour the milk and cream into the same pan, add the cinnamon, vanilla pod and orange peel. Bring to just below boiling point over a low–medium heat, then remove from the heat and leave to infuse for 30 minutes.

2 Tip the brioche pieces into a bowl. Pour the melted butter over and stir to coat. Scatter one third of the brioche into the tin, top with half each of the raisins and chocolate. Arrange another third of the brioche on top and the remaining raisins (and any residual Madeira) and chocolate. Cover with the remaining brioche.

3 Whisk the eggs, yolks and sugar in the brioche bowl until combined. Strain the infused milk and cream into the bowl and whisk to combine. Ladle the custard over the brioche and leave it to soak for 30 minutes. Heat the oven to 180°C/160°C fan/Gas 4.

4 Loosely cover the pudding with foil and bake for 25 minutes, until the custard just sets. Remove the foil, scatter with the demerara sugar and bake for another 10 minutes, until the top starts to crisp. Leave to cool, cover and chill until ready to serve.

5 **Make the custard.** Put the milk, cream, bay leaf and cinnamon in a pan on a low–medium heat and bring to the boil. Immediately remove from the heat and leave to infuse for 20 minutes.

6 Tip half of the sugar into a small pan, add 1 tablespoon of water and place over a low heat to dissolve the sugar, swirling the pan. Bring to the boil and cook to an amber-coloured caramel. Remove from the heat and stir in the orange juice. Return to a low heat, bring to the boil and cook, stirring occasionally, to reduce by half.

7 In a bowl, whisk the egg yolks with the remaining sugar. Reheat the milk and cream to just below boiling and add the orange caramel. Whisking continuously, pour half of the hot milk mixture onto the egg yolks. Return it to the pan and cook on a low–medium heat, stirring, until the custard coats a spoon (but do not let the mixture boil). Strain into a jug, cover and set aside.

8 **Assemble the dessert.** Heat the oven to 200°C/180°C fan/Gas 6. Cut the cold pudding into eight equal portions. Tip the 4 tablespoons of caster sugar onto a plate and press each portion in the sugar to coat. Bake the puddings on the lined baking tray for 20 minutes, until hot and caramelising. Gently reheat the custard and pour it onto serving plates, top with the puddings and serve with any extra custard in a jug for pouring over.

Black Forest chocolate mousse cake

Serves: 10
Hands on: 2 hours + chilling
Bake: 10 mins

FOR THE SPONGES
3 eggs
100g caster sugar
50g ground almonds
25g plain flour
25g cocoa powder
pinch of salt
25g unsalted butter

FOR THE KIRSCH SYRUP
50g caster sugar
50ml kirsch

FOR THE MOUSSE
200g 70% dark chocolate, chopped
350ml double cream
75g caster sugar
4 egg yolks
1 tsp vanilla paste
100g well-drained Amarena
    cherries in syrup, halved
100g well-drained good-quality
    tinned pitted cherries, halved

FOR THE GLAZE
125ml double cream
50ml whole milk
40g liquid glucose
125g 70% dark chocolate,
    finely chopped

TO DECORATE
150ml double cream
1 tsp vanilla paste
50g 70% dark chocolate,
    finely grated
Amarena or fresh cherries
    with their stalks

Continues overleaf

This reinvention of a classic Black Forest gâteau is pure indulgence. The cake layers are separated by a generous layer of chocolate mousse studded with two types of cherry. The Amarena cherries, from Italy, are small and dark, and in thick syrup. If you can't find them, you could use double the quantity of tinned, or try using cherries in kirsch instead.

. . . .

1 **Make the sponges.** Heat the oven to 190°C/170°C fan/Gas 5. Whisk the eggs with the caster sugar in a stand mixer fitted with the whisk, on medium speed for 2–3 minutes, until pale and the mixture leaves a ribbon trail when you lift the whisk. Sift the ground almonds, flour, cocoa powder and salt into the bowl and fold them in using a large metal spoon, until almost combined.

2 Melt the butter in a small pan, then pour it into the bowl and fold it in until combined (take care not to overmix and deflate the mixture).

3 Divide the mixture equally between the prepared tins, spread it level using an offset palette knife and bake the sponges on the middle shelf for 8–9 minutes, until just firm to the touch. Leave the sponges to cool in the tins for 2–3 minutes, then turn them out onto a wire rack (leave the baking paper in place), to cool completely.

4 **Make the kirsch syrup.** While the sponges are cooling, gently heat the sugar and kirsch with 50ml of water in a small pan until the sugar dissolves, swirling the pan occasionally. Increase the heat and bring to the boil, then turn the heat down and simmer for 2–3 minutes, until the syrup reduces by half. Pour the syrup into a small bowl and set it aside to cool slightly.

5 **Begin assembling the cake.** Line the sides of the springform tin with the acetate strip. Place one sponge layer in the bottom of the tin, baking paper-side down and brush the top with the kirsch syrup. Set aside.

6 **Make the mousse.** Melt the chocolate in a heatproof bowl set over a pan of gently simmering water. Stir until smooth, then remove from the heat. Meanwhile, whip the cream to soft peaks and chill until needed.

7 Tip the sugar into a small pan, add 3 tablespoons of water and place on a low heat to dissolve the sugar, swirling the pan occasionally. Bring to the boil, then turn the heat down and simmer for 5 minutes, until the syrup reaches 118°C on the sugar thermometer.

Continues overleaf

Black Forest chocolate mousse cake
continued

You will need
20cm sandwich tins x 2,
   greased, then base-lined
   with baking paper
20cm, deep springform tin
65 x 8cm acetate strip
sugar thermometer
20cm cake board or plate
medium piping bag fitted
   with a medium star nozzle

8 Meanwhile, using an electric hand whisk, beat the egg yolks and vanilla in a large bowl until thickened and paler in colour. Slowly and carefully, pour the hot syrup onto the yolks, whisking continuously until combined. Increase the speed and continue whisking until the mixture is very thick, pale and mousse-like, scraping down the inside of the bowl from time to time.

9 Using a rubber spatula, fold in the melted chocolate, then mix in one-third of the whipped cream until smooth. Fold in the remaining cream in a further two batches.

10 **Finish assembling the cake.** Spoon half of the chocolate mousse mixture into the tin on top of the sponge layer and spread it level. Mix both types of cherry together and scatter them over the mousse, leaving a 1cm border around the edge. Cover the cherries with the remaining mousse and spread it level.

11 Brush the top of the second sponge layer with syrup and place this on top of the mousse, baking paper uppermost. Gently press the layers together, cover and chill for at least 4 hours to set.

12 **Make the glaze.** When you're ready to finish the cake, gently heat the cream, milk and glucose in a small pan until almost bubbling. Tip the chocolate into a large bowl, add the hot cream mixture, leave for 1 minute and stir until the chocolate melts and is silky smooth. Leave the glaze to cool for 5 minutes.

13 Remove the cake from the tin and carefully peel off the acetate strip and the top disc of baking paper. Place the cake board or cake plate on the top of the cake and carefully invert, placing the inverted cake onto a cooling rack or upturned bowl. Peel off the baking paper, then slowly spoon the glaze over the top and down the sides of the cake to coat it smoothly and evenly. Chill the cake for 30 minutes.

14 **Decorate and finish the cake.** Whip the cream with the vanilla to medium-firm peaks, then spoon it into the piping bag fitted with a star nozzle.

15 Use a palette knife to coat the sides of the cake with the grated chocolate, leaving a sprinkling of chocolate to decorate the top.

16 Pipe the cream in swirls around the top edge of the cake and sprinkle them with the remaining grated chocolate. Chill the cake for a further 30 minutes, then decorate with the cherries to finish.

8
Free-from

Vegan Coffee & walnut cake

Serves: 10
Hands on: 2 hours + chilling
Bake: 35 mins

FOR THE SPONGES
150ml sunflower oil
200g plain vegan yogurt
200ml plant milk (oat or nut)
2 tbsp agave nectar
2 tsp cider vinegar
1 tsp vanilla paste
4 tsp instant espresso powder,
    dissolved in 3 tsp boiling water
450g self-raising flour
1½ tsp baking powder
1 tsp bicarbonate of soda
pinch of salt
225g golden caster sugar

FOR THE COFFEE SYRUP
2 tbsp golden caster sugar
1 tsp instant espresso powder
1 tsp vanilla paste
2 tbsp just-boiled water

FOR THE PRALINE
100g caster sugar
100g walnuts, roughly chopped

FOR THE FROSTING
250g vegan butter
500g icing sugar, sifted
4 tsp instant espresso powder
    dissolved in 3 tsp just-boiled water
dairy-free chocolate-coated coffee
    beans, to finish

You will need
18cm round cake tins x 3, greased,
    then base-lined with baking paper
baking sheet, lined with baking paper
25cm cake plate or board
medium piping bag fitted with
    a medium star nozzle
cake scraper

A sophisticated take on the classic coffee cake, in this recipe the nuts are turned into praline, which is scattered in the layers, and also broken into shards to decorate.

. . . .

1 **Make the sponges.** Heat the oven to 180°C/160°C fan/Gas 4. In a jug, whisk together the oil, yogurt, milk, agave, vinegar, vanilla and coffee. Sift the flour, baking powder, bicarbonate of soda and salt into a large bowl. Add the sugar, then make a well in the middle of the dry ingredients and add the wet mixture. Using a balloon whisk, mix to combine thoroughly.

2 Divide the mixture equally between the tins and spread it level. Bake for 30–35 minutes, until risen, and a skewer inserted into the centres comes out clean. Leave to cool in the tins for 5 minutes, then turn out onto a wire rack to cool completely.

3 **Make the coffee syrup.** Mix all the syrup ingredients in a small bowl until the sugar dissolves, then leave to cool.

4 **Make the praline.** Tip the sugar into a small pan and add 2 tablespoons of water. Place on a low–medium heat and heat to dissolve the sugar. Bring the syrup to the boil and cook, swirling the pan, until it turns amber. Stir in the walnuts and cook for a further 20 seconds. Scoop the mixture onto the lined baking sheet, spread it level and leave to cool. When the praline is cold, break off one-third and blitz it in a food processor to finely chop.

5 **Make the frosting.** Beat the vegan butter in a stand mixer fitted with a beater, on medium speed for 3–4 minutes, until pale and creamy. Gradually add the icing sugar, mixing well between each addition, then mix in the coffee.

6 **Assemble the cake.** Level the tops of the sponges, if needed. Place one sponge on the cake plate or board and brush the top with coffee syrup. Spread 4 tablespoons of frosting over the top and scatter with one-third of the crushed praline. Top with the second sponge and repeat the layering, ending with the third sponge. Chill for 15 minutes.

7 Spoon 4 tablespoons of frosting into the piping bag. Spread the top and sides of the cake with the remaining frosting in the bowl, then use the cake scraper to remove the excess from the sides, leaving the cake with a thin layer of frosting and visible layers (semi-naked). Use a palette knife to smooth the frosting on top.

8 Add any leftover frosting to the piping bag and pipe rosettes on top of the cake. Press the remaining crushed praline around the base and break the large praline chunk into shards. Press the shards into the rosettes, then scatter with coffee beans to finish.

Gluten-free
Seeded bagels

Makes: 8
Hands on: 25 mins + rising
Bake: 30 mins

150g brown rice flour
125g oat flour, plus extra
    for dusting
125g tapioca flour
100g potato flour
20g psyllium husk powder
1 tbsp ground flaxseed
2 tsp caster sugar
7g fast-action dried yeast
1 tsp salt
300ml whole milk
200–225ml lukewarm water
1 tbsp molasses syrup
1 egg, beaten, to glaze
4 tbsp mixed seeds

You will need
large baking sheet,
    lined with baking paper

These seeded gluten-free bagels are flavoursome, soft and chewy – everything you want from a bagel, and more. There's no kneading involved, so they're super-quick to make, too.

. . . .

1 **Make the dough.** Using a balloon whisk, mix all the flours, psyllium husk, flaxseed, sugar, yeast and salt in the bowl of a stand mixer. Attach the bowl to the mixer fitted with the dough hook and make a well in the middle of the dry ingredients.

2 Heat the milk until lukewarm and pour it into the bowl with 200ml of the lukewarm water. Mix on low for 1 minute, until the dough is smooth and the ingredients combined – add a further 25ml lukewarm water if the dough looks dry. (You don't need to knead the dough, because there's no call for developing any gluten.)

3 **Shape the dough.** Lightly dust the work surface with oat flour and turn the dough out of the bowl. Divide it into 8 equal pieces, shape each one into a smooth ball and place it on the lined baking sheet, spacing the bagels well apart. Working with one piece at a time, use a floured finger to press a hole into the middle of the dough ball and swirl it around to create a ring of dough with a 3–4cm hole in the centre.

4 Loosely cover the bagels with a tea towel and leave them at room temperature for 1 hour, until risen and puffy. Meanwhile, heat the oven to 190°C/170°C fan/Gas 5 and bring a large pan of water to the simmer. Stir in the molasses syrup.

5 **Poach the bagels.** Drop the risen bagels into the pan of simmering water in batches of two or three, depending on the size of the pan. (They need to cook in a single layer and, because they puff up a little as they poach, allow space between each one.) Cook the bagels for 1 minute on each side, then remove them with a fish slice and return them to the lined baking sheet, rounded-side up. Poach the remaining bagels and arrange them spaced apart on the baking sheet.

6 **Bake the bagels.** Brush the top of the bagels with beaten egg and scatter with the seeds. Bake for 30 minutes, until risen, golden and the underside of each bagel sounds hollow when tapped. Place them on a wire rack to cool before serving.

Vegan Blueberry & lemon cupcakes

> I believe the beauty of baking is being able to share the deliciousness with everybody. From celebrations to an afternoon tea to lunchboxes, my moist and fluffy vegan cupcakes are the perfect treat for every occasion.

. . . .

Makes: 12
Hands on: 25 mins
Bake: 25 mins

FOR THE CUPCAKES
275g plain flour
3 tsp baking powder
225g caster sugar
50g unsweetened
    desiccated coconut
pinch of salt
250ml plant-based milk
    (almond, soy or oat)
125ml sunflower oil
1 tsp vanilla extract
1 tsp finely grated
    unwaxed lemon zest
125g blueberries

FOR THE FROSTING
125g blueberries
1 tbsp lemon juice
2 tbsp caster sugar
250g vegan butter,
    cubed and softened
500g icing sugar, sifted
1 tbsp freeze-dried raspberry
    pieces, to decorate

You will need
12-hole muffin tin,
    lined with paper cases
large piping bag fitted
    with a medium star nozzle

1 **Make the cupcakes.** Heat the oven to 180°C/160°C fan/Gas 4. Sift the flour and baking powder into a large bowl. Add the sugar, coconut and salt and stir with a balloon whisk until combined.

2 Make a well in the middle of the dry ingredients, add the milk, oil, vanilla and lemon zest and mix until just combined. Fold through the blueberries and divide the mixture between the lined holes in the muffin tin.

3 Bake the muffins for 25 minutes, until risen, golden, and a skewer inserted into the middle of the cupcakes comes out clean. Leave to cool in the tin for 5 minutes, then transfer to a wire rack to cool completely.

4 **Make the buttercream frosting.** While the cupcakes are cooling, tip the blueberries into a small pan, add the lemon juice and caster sugar and cook on a low–medium heat, stirring often, for 5 minutes, until the berries are soft, juicy and jammy. Press the blueberry mixture through a fine-mesh sieve into a bowl and leave the compôte to cool to room temperature.

5 Beat the butter in a stand mixer fitted with the beater, on medium speed for 3 minutes, until light and creamy. A third at a time, add the icing sugar, beating on low speed until the mixture is light and fluffy. Add the blueberry compôte and mix again until you have a combined, even colour.

6 Spoon the frosting into the piping bag fitted with the star nozzle. Pipe a swirl of frosting on the top of each cupcake, then decorate with a sprinkling of freeze-dried raspberry pieces.

Dairy & gluten-free Lemon cake

Serves: 8
Hands on: 1½ hours
Bake: 35 mins

FOR THE SPONGE
4 eggs, separated
200g caster sugar
125ml light olive oil
100g plain vegan yogurt
juice and finely grated zest
   of 2 unwaxed lemons
175g ground almonds
25g cornflour
25g coconut or brown
   rice flour
3 tsp baking powder
pinch of salt

FOR THE GLAZE
juice and finely grated zest
   of 1 unwaxed lemon
125g icing sugar, sifted,
   plus extra for dusting

FOR THE SPICED CANDIED LEMON SLICES
150g caster sugar
1 star anise
1 cinnamon stick
2 unwaxed lemons,
   thinly sliced into rounds,
   then cut in half

You will need
23cm ridged bundt tin,
   greased with melted vegan
   butter and dusted with
   gluten-free plain flour

This cake is based on an Italian lemon torta caprese, which is made with almond flour and so 'naturally' gluten-free. For this recipe we have baked it in a bundt tin, but it will work perfectly in a 23cm cake tin, too.

. . . .

1 Heat the oven to 180°C/160°C fan/Gas 4.

2 **Make the sponge.** Whisk the egg yolks and sugar in a stand mixer fitted with the whisk, on medium–high speed for 2 minutes, until light and mousse-like.

3 Mix the olive oil, yogurt, lemon juice and zest in a jug. In a steady stream and on low speed, add this mixture to the bowl with the eggs and sugar. Scrape down the inside of the bowl, then sift in the ground almonds, cornflour, coconut or brown rice flour, baking powder and salt and mix on low to combine.

4 Using a hand-held electric whisk, whisk the egg whites to stiff peaks and gently fold them into the mixture.

5 Pour the mixture into the prepared tin and spread it level with a palette knife. Bake on the middle shelf for 30–35 minutes, until risen and golden, and a skewer inserted into the centre comes out clean. Leave the cake in the tin for 2–3 minutes, then turn it out onto a wire rack. Keep the oven on.

6 **Make the glaze.** While the cake is still warm, simmer the lemon juice and zest in a small pan for 30 seconds to reduce it slightly. Remove from the heat and stir in the icing sugar until dissolved. Leave the glaze to cool and thicken slightly.

7 Brush the top and the sides of the warm cake with the glaze, leave it for 5 minutes, then brush it again. Leave it for 5 minutes, then slide the cake back into the oven. Turn off the heat and leave the cake inside for 5 minutes, until the glaze is translucent.

8 **Make the candied lemon slices.** Meanwhile, tip the sugar into a sauté pan or large frying pan, add the star anise and cinnamon stick and 150ml of water. Place the pan on a low heat and stir to dissolve the sugar. Add the lemon slices and cook on a low heat, stirring gently from time to time, for 40 minutes, until the pith is translucent, and the lemon slices are candied and sticky. Add a splash more water if the syrup reduces too much before the lemon slices are candied. Using a fork, lift the lemon slices out of the syrup onto a sheet of baking paper and leave them to dry and cool for 10 minutes, or until needed.

9 To finish the cake, place the candied lemon slices around the top of the cake, dust with icing sugar, and serve.

Vegan
Tropical fruit tart

The filling in this tart is a luxurious and rich vegan crème pâtissière that's laced with coconut cream, which lends itself so beautifully to the topping of exotic fruits.

• • • • • • • • • • • •

Serves: 6–8
Hands on: 1½ hours
   + infusing and chilling
Bake: 30 mins

FOR THE PASTRY
200g plain flour
pinch of salt
100g vegan unsalted butter,
   cubed and chilled
35g icing sugar, sifted,
   plus extra for dusting
2 tbsp plant milk
   (oat, rice, almond or soy)

FOR THE CRÈME PÂTISSIÈRE
450ml plant milk
1 tsp vanilla paste or
   ½ vanilla pod, split
1 strip of unwaxed lemon peel
pinch of saffron
1 cinnamon stick
50g cornflour
75g caster sugar
1 tbsp coconut cream
25g unsalted vegan butter

FOR THE TOPPING
1 large ripe mango, peeled,
   stone removed and cut
   into bite-sized pieces
2 kiwi fruit, peeled and cut
   into bite-sized pieces
3 ripe figs, cut into thin wedges
3 tbsp pomegranate seeds
scooped pulp of 1 large passion fruit
2 tbsp toasted coconut chips
   and mint leaves, to decorate

FOR THE GLAZE
1 tbsp arrowroot
200ml pineapple juice

You will need
20cm loose-bottomed
   fluted tart tin
baking beans

1 **Make the pastry.** Mix the flour and salt in a large bowl. Using your fingertips, rub in the butter until the mixture resembles breadcrumbs, with only small flecks of butter remaining. Mix in the icing sugar. Stir in the milk with a table knife, then use your hands to gather the pastry into a neat ball. Flatten it into a disc, then wrap and chill it for 1 hour, until firm.

2 **Start the crème pâtissière.** Meanwhile, heat the milk with the vanilla, lemon peel, saffron and cinnamon in a pan on a low–medium heat and bring to just below boiling. Remove the pan from the heat and leave to infuse for 30 minutes to 1 hour.

3 **Make the tart case.** Lightly flour the work surface and roll out the pastry into a neat 30cm disc, about 3mm thick. Use this to line the base and sides of the tart tin, pressing the pastry into the corners. Trim the excess, prick the base and chill for 20 minutes. Meanwhile, heat the oven to 180°C/160°C fan/Gas 4 and place a baking sheet in the oven to heat up.

4 Line the pastry case with baking paper and fill it with baking beans. Place the tart tin on the hot baking sheet and bake for 25 minutes, until the edges of the pastry are pale golden. Remove the paper and beans and bake for a further 5 minutes to cook the base. Leave to cool.

5 **Finish the crème pâtissière.** In a bowl, combine the cornflour and caster sugar. Strain the infused milk, then reheat it to almost boiling. Whisking continuously, pour half of the hot milk into the bowl with the cornflour and mix to a smooth paste. Return the mixture to the pan with the remaining milk and cook on a low–medium heat, whisking continuously until the crème thickens and you can no longer taste the cornflour. Whisk in the coconut cream and vegan butter. Pour the crème pât into a clean bowl, cover the surface with a disc of baking paper and leave to cool.

6 **Assemble the tart.** Remove the pastry case from the tin and place it on a serving plate. Whisk the crème pât until smooth, then spoon it into the pastry case and spread it level. Arrange all the fruit on top and spoon over the passion fruit pulp.

7 **Make the glaze.** Combine the arrowroot with a little of the pineapple juice in a small pan to make a paste. Add the remaining juice and bring the mixture to the boil, stirring until the glaze is clear and thickened. Leave to cool slightly, then brush or spoon it over the fruit. Decorate the tart with coconut chips and mint.

Gluten-free
Seeded bread

Makes: 1 large loaf
Hands on: 30 mins + rising
Bake: 65 minutes

30g psyllium husk (not powder)
600ml lukewarm water
150g oat flour
50g buckwheat flour
150g potato starch
125g millet flour
7g fast-action dried yeast
1½ tsp salt
1 tbsp honey or maple syrup
2 tsp cider vinegar
50g blanched hazelnuts,
    roughly chopped
50g sunflower seeds
50g pumpkin seeds

TO FINISH
1 tbsp whole milk,
    to glaze (optional)
1 tbsp sesame seeds

You will need
900g loaf tin, greased,
    then base and ends lined
    with a strip of baking paper
proving bag (optional)
large roasting tin

This tasty, crusty, gluten-free loaf makes excellent toast – and is especially moreish spread with peanut butter. Adapt the seeds and nuts to your preference and even add a handful of raisins or currants to the dough, if you like.

1 **Make the dough.** In a large bowl, whisk together the psyllium husk with 350ml of the lukewarm water until combined, then set aside for 1 minute, until it forms a gel.

2 Using a balloon whisk, mix the oat flour, buckwheat flour, potato starch, millet flour, yeast and salt in the bowl of a stand mixer. Make a well in the middle of the dry ingredients and add the psyllium gel, and the honey, vinegar and the remaining 250ml of lukewarm water. Attach the bowl to the stand mixer fitted with the dough hook and mix on low speed until combined. Scrape down the inside of the bowl, then turn the speed up to medium and mix for a further 2 minutes, until the dough is smooth and cleanly leaves the sides of the bowl. Add the hazelnuts and both types of seed and mix again to combine.

3 **Shape the dough.** Lightly flour the work surface, tip out the dough and quickly shape it into a rectangular loaf. Place the loaf in the lined tin, smooth side up, loosely cover with a proving bag or clean tea towel and leave it at a cool room temperature for about 1½ hours, until the dough is puffy, has almost doubled in size and has risen above the sides of the tin.

4 About 20 minutes before the dough is ready, heat the oven to 240°C/220°C fan/Gas 8. Place an oven shelf in the bottom third of the oven and a roasting tin underneath it on the oven floor.

5 Gently brush the top of the proved loaf with milk, if using, or water and scatter with the sesame seeds. Pour boiling water to a depth of 2cm into the roasting tin on the floor of the oven, and slide the loaf tin onto the shelf above.

6 **Bake the loaf.** Bake your bread for 15 minutes, then reduce the oven to 220°C/200°C fan/Gas 7 and cook for a further 45–50 minutes, until the loaf is risen, crusty and deep golden brown. Keep an eye during baking and if the loaf is browning too fast, loosely cover it with foil for the last 20 minutes. Turn the bread out of the tin and place it on a wire rack to cool completely before slicing.

Vegan
Caramelly chocolate cupcakes

These vegan cupcakes are deeply chocolatey with a delicate crumb and topped with a generous swoosh of buttercream. Panela is raw, unrefined cane sugar with an especially caramel flavour, but you can use light muscovado or light brown soft sugar, if you prefer.

. . . .

Makes: 12
Hands on: 25 mins + cooling
Bake: 25 mins

FOR THE CUPCAKES
225ml soy or oat milk
1 tbsp cider vinegar
3 tbsp plain vegan yogurt
75ml sunflower oil
1 tsp vanilla extract
100g panela organic sugar
100g caster sugar
200g plain flour
1 tsp bicarbonate of soda
40g unsweetened cocoa powder
pinch of salt

FOR THE FROSTING
150g unsalted vegan
    butter, softened
350g icing sugar, sifted
5 tbsp unsweetened
    cocoa powder, sifted
12 blackberries, to decorate

You will need
12-hole muffin tin,
    lined with paper cases

1 **Make the cupcakes.** Heat the oven to 180°C/160°C fan/Gas 4. In a jug, whisk the soy or oat milk with the vinegar and yogurt. Add the oil and vanilla and mix to combine.

2 In a large bowl, combine both types of sugar, then mix in the yogurt mixture using a balloon whisk. Sift the flour, bicarbonate of soda, cocoa powder and salt into the bowl and whisk again until smooth.

3 Pour the mixture into a large measuring jug and divide it equally between the paper cases, filling each case two-thirds full. Bake for 25 minutes, until risen and a wooden skewer inserted into the middle of each cupcake comes out clean. Leave the cupcakes to cool in the tin for 5 minutes, then transfer them to a wire rack to cool completely.

4 **Make the frosting.** While the cupcakes are cooling, beat the vegan butter in a stand mixer fitted with the beater, on low–medium speed for 2 minutes, until light and soft. Add one-third of the icing sugar and mix slowly to combine. Add the remaining icing sugar in two batches and mix, scraping down the inside of the bowl from time to time, until smooth and creamy.

5 Add the cocoa powder to the frosting and mix again until smooth. Cover the top of each cupcake with the frosting, using a palette knife to create swirls. Decorate with a blackberry to finish.

Vegan
Mini pavlovas

Perfect vegan pavlovas! The trick in this recipe is to reduce the aquafaba before you whisk it, which makes the mixture more stable and so the meringue more pipeable.

. . . .

Makes: 8
Hands on: 20 mins + cooling
Bake: 1 hour

FOR THE MERINGUE
aquafaba from 2 x 400g cans
    of chickpeas (about 250ml)
¼ tsp cream of tartar
pinch of salt
200g caster sugar
1 tsp vanilla paste
1 tsp cornflour
1 tsp white wine vinegar

FOR THE TOPPING
220ml vegan double cream
scooped pulp from
    2 passion fruits
1 tsp vanilla paste
1 tbsp icing sugar, sifted
1 tsp finely grated unwaxed
    lemon zest
200g strawberries,
    hulled and sliced
100g raspberries
100g blueberries

You will need
10cm plain cutter
large baking sheet,
    lined with baking paper
large piping bag fitted
    with an open star nozzle

1 Using the 10cm plain cutter as a guide, draw 8 evenly spaced circles on the sheet of baking paper lining the baking sheet. Turn the paper drawn-side down.

2 **Make the meringue.** Bring the aquafaba to the boil in a small pan, then turn the heat down and simmer until reduced to 150ml. Pour it into the bowl of a stand mixer and leave to cool.

3 Heat the oven to 120°C/100°C fan/Gas ¾.

4 Whisk the cooled aquafaba with the cream of tartar and salt in the stand mixer fitted with the whisk, on medium speed for 4 minutes, until the aquafaba forms stiff peaks. A tablespoon at a time, add the caster sugar, whisking well between each addition and scraping down the inside of the bowl from time to time, until the meringue is silky smooth, glossy and the sugar has dissolved. Whisk in the vanilla until combined.

5 In a small bowl, mix the cornflour with the white wine vinegar, then add the mixture to the meringue and whisk again on medium speed for another 30 seconds to combine.

6 Spoon the mixture into the piping bag fitted with an open star nozzle and pipe 8 meringues on the lined baking sheet, using the drawn circles as a guide and leaving a little space between each one. Bake the meringues for 1 hour, until crisp and firm on the outside. Turn the oven off and leave the meringues in the oven to cool and dry for at least 4 hours, or ideally overnight.

7 **Make the topping.** Whisk the vegan cream with the pulp of one passion fruit, and the vanilla, icing sugar and lemon zest until the cream holds firm peaks.

8 **Assemble the pavlovas.** Carefully place one mini pavlova onto each serving plate. Spoon equal amounts of the whipped cream mixture in the centre of each one and arrange the strawberries, raspberries and blueberries on top. Spoon the remaining passion fruit pulp over and serve immediately.

Gluten-free
Chocolate orange macarons

Makes: 30
Hands on: 30 mins + resting
Bake: 13 mins

FOR THE MACARON SHELLS
175g ground almonds
175g icing sugar, sifted
150g egg whites (about 4–5)
¼ tsp orange food-colouring paste
1 tsp orange extract
pinch of salt
175g caster sugar

FOR THE GANACHE FILLING
150g 70% dark chocolate,
    finely chopped, plus 25g
    to decorate
100ml double cream
1 tbsp runny honey
1 tsp finely grated unwaxed
    orange zest
1 tbsp bronze sprinkles,
    to decorate

You will need
4cm plain cutter
2 large baking sheets, lined with
    baking paper and drawn with
    30 evenly spaced 4cm-diameter
    circles (use the cutter as a guide)
large piping bag fitted with
    a medium plain nozzle
medium piping bag fitted
    with a medium plain nozzle
small piping bag fitted with
    a small writing nozzle

Practice and patience make perfect macarons. These have a chocolate-orange flavour, delicate piping and dainty bronze sprinkles to elevate them to patisserie status.

· · · · · · · · · · · · ·

1 **Make the macaron shells.** Blitz the ground almonds and icing sugar in a food processor for 30 seconds, until combined. Add 75g of the egg whites, and the food colouring and orange extract and pulse to a smooth, thick paste. Spoon the mixture into a bowl.

2 Tip the remaining egg whites and the salt into a heatproof glass bowl. Add the sugar and 2 teaspoons of water. Set the bowl over a pan of simmering water and beat with a balloon whisk for 3–4 minutes, until the mixture just holds a ribbon trail. Remove from the heat and, using an electric hand whisk, beat on low–medium speed for 2–3 minutes, until thick and mousse-like.

3 Using a silicone spatula, fold one quarter of the meringue mixture into the almond mixture to almost combine, then return it to the meringue and fold in until smooth and combined. The macaron mixture should resemble thick, molten lava and hold a ribbon trail for 5 seconds when you lift the spatula.

4 Working quickly, scoop the macaron mixture into the large piping bag fitted with a medium plain nozzle, twist the end to seal and pipe 30 equal-sized macarons onto each lined baking sheet, using the circles as a guide. Tap the baking sheets on the work surface to pop any air bubbles, then leave the macarons uncovered for 30 minutes, until a light skin forms on the surface of each one. Heat the oven to 170°C/150°C fan/Gas 3.

5 Once the macarons have rested, bake them in the centre of the oven for 13 minutes, until risen, and crisp on top with a well-defined 'foot'. Remove from the oven and leave to cool completely.

6 **Make the ganache.** Tip the chocolate into a bowl. Heat the cream with the honey and the orange zest in a small pan until only just boiling. Stir, then pour this over the chocolate. Leave for 30 seconds, then stir until smooth. Whisk with a balloon whisk until cool and thick enough to pipe. Spoon the ganache into the medium piping bag with the medium plain nozzle. Set aside.

7 **Make the decoration.** Melt the 25g of chocolate, then pour it into the small piping bag. Pipe four thin lines in a criss-cross pattern and 2 or 3 small dots on top of one tray of the macarons, scatter over the sprinkles and leave to set.

8 **Assemble the macarons.** Turn the undecorated shells flat-side up. Pipe a generous teaspoon of ganache in the middle of each, then top with a decorated shell, flat-side down. The macarons will store in an airtight box in the fridge for 3–4 days.

Original kitchen classics

Every recipe in this book so far has been a kitchen classic with
a new and exciting twist – whether that's in its flavour, its decoration
or its size, or by some other delicious reimagining. Over the following
pages, we pay homage to one recipe from each signature theme that
we think perfectly represents an *original* kitchen classic. These recipes
are the beginnings. Use them just as they are, or as a blank canvas to
inspire your own baking reinventions.

CAKE

Victoria sponge

Serves: 8
Hands on: 20 mins
Bake: 30 mins

FOR THE SPONGES
200g unsalted butter, softened
200g golden caster sugar
1 tsp vanilla paste
4 eggs, beaten
200g self-raising flour, sifted
1 tsp baking powder
150g homemade or good-quality
   strawberry jam
icing sugar, for dusting

FOR THE BUTTERCREAM
100g unsalted butter, softened
200g icing sugar, sifted
½ tsp vanilla paste

You will need
20cm sandwich tins x 2,
   greased, then base-lined
   with baking paper
large disposable piping
   bag (optional)

The Victoria sponge is so-named for Queen Victoria, who was said to be an early proponent of formal afternoon tea. However, its origins are far earlier than her lifetime – some claim that a recipe for 'biscuit bread' in Gervase Markham's book *The English Housewife* (1615) is the earliest written proof we have for this most quintessential of British cakes.

. . . .

1 Heat the oven to 180°C/160°C fan/Gas 4 .

2 **Make the sponges.** Beat the butter, sugar and vanilla in a stand mixer fitted with the beater, on medium speed for 5–6 minutes, scraping down the inside of the bowl from time to time, until the mixture is pale and creamy.

3 A little at a time, add the eggs, beating well between each addition until well combined. If the mixture curdles, add 1 tablespoon of the flour and combine again.

4 In a separate bowl, whisk together the flour and baking powder. Then, fold the dry ingredients through the wet ingredients, until just incorporated.

5 Divide the cake mixture equally between the two sandwich tins. Bake for 25–30 minutes, until golden and springy and a skewer inserted into the centres comes out clean. Cool the sponges in the tins for 5 minutes, then turn out onto a wire rack to cool completely.

6 **Make the buttercream.** Beat the butter, icing sugar and vanilla together in a stand mixer fitted with the beater, on medium speed for 1–2 minutes, scraping down the inside of the bowl a few times, until fluffy.

7 **Assemble the cake.** Place one of the cooled sponges upside down on a cake plate or stand. Spread with the jam, then spread the buttercream over the top. Alternatively, fill the piping bag with the buttercream and snip a 1cm hole in the end. Pipe the buttercream in little blobs around the outside edge of the sponge, then use a palette knife to swirl it in towards the centre to completely cover.

8 Place the second sponge on top. Press the sponges gently together, then dust with icing sugar before serving.

Shortbread biscuits

Makes: 16
Hands on: 15 mins + chilling
Bake: 20 mins

125g unsalted butter
55g caster sugar,
    plus extra to sprinkle
200g plain flour

You will need
6cm fluted biscuit cutter
baking sheet, lined
    with baking paper

The definitive biscuit for a cup of tea has to be shortbread, the origins of which date back to the 12th century (although that was made using leftover bread dough). This recipe is faithful to the traditions of Scottish shortbread, which is made with just three ingredients: butter, sugar and flour.

. . . .

1 **Make the dough.** Put the butter and sugar in the bowl of a food processor and blitz until well combined. Add the flour and pulse briefly until the mixture resembles breadcrumbs.

2 Tip out the mixture onto a work surface and gently bring it together, then knead it into a dough. Once the dough is formed, wrap it and chill for 30 minutes. Heat the oven to 170°C/150°C fan/Gas 3.

3 **Stamp out the biscuits.** Lightly flour the work surface and roll out the dough until it is about 3mm thick. Use the 6cm fluted cutter to stamp out 16 biscuits, re-rolling the trimmings as necessary.

4 Place the biscuits on the lined baking sheet and chill for another 5 minutes, then use a fork to prick a few lines of holes in the centre of each.

5 **Bake the biscuits.** Sprinkle the biscuits with a little caster sugar and bake them for 15–20 minutes, or until lightly golden.

6 Remove the biscuits from the oven and leave them to cool on the baking sheet for 10 minutes. Then, transfer them to a wire rack to cool completely. They will keep in a sealed container for up to 1 week.

White bloomer

The 19th- or 20th-century name 'bloomer' is thought to refer to the fact that a traditional bloomer loaf isn't made in a tin, but rather the dough is left to 'bloom' and rise tin-free.

. . . .

Makes: 1 loaf
Hands on: 30 mins + rising
Bake: 35 mins

500g strong white bread flour,
   plus extra for dusting
7g fast-action dried yeast
1½ tsp salt
325–375ml lukewarm water
1 tbsp olive oil
1 tbsp poppy seeds (optional)

You will need
large baking tray, dusted
   with flour or semolina
sharp knife or scalpel

1 **Make the dough.** Mix the flour, yeast and salt together in a bowl. Make a well and pour in 300ml of the lukewarm water and all the oil. Mix vigorously with a round-bladed knife until the mixture comes together in a craggy, lumpy dough. Add enough of the remaining water to achieve a soft but not sticky dough.

2 Tip out the dough onto a lightly floured work surface and bring it together into a ball. Knead it for 8–10 minutes, until smooth and elastic (it should bounce straight back when gently pressed). Form the dough into a ball and place it in an oiled bowl. Cover with a damp cloth and leave it in a warm place for 45 minutes to 1 hour, or until doubled in size.

3 Turn out the risen dough onto a lightly floured work surface. Gently knead it two or three times to knock it back. Avoid over-kneading at this stage, or the bread will lose its lightness.

4 **Shape the loaf.** Flatten the dough into a 25 x 20cm rectangle, patting it out with your fingers and gently pulling the edges. Fold both short ends into the centre (like folding a business letter), then turn the dough through 90 degrees. Flatten the dough once more into a rectangle, then, starting from one of the short ends, roll it up into a tight cylinder. Seal both ends by pressing down firmly with the palm of each hand, then tuck the ends under the loaf. You should be left with a taught, oval-shaped loaf.

5 **Prove the loaf.** Transfer the shaped loaf to the prepared baking tray, seam-side downwards. Sprinkle over the poppy seeds, if using, then dust lightly with flour. Using the sharp knife or scalpel, make three 2cm-deep slashes in the top of the loaf at an angle. Cover the loaf with a clean tea towel and set it aside to prove for 35–45 minutes, until almost doubled in size. Meanwhile, heat the oven to 230°C/210°C fan/Gas 8 and put an empty roasting tin in the bottom of the oven to heat up.

6 **Bake the loaf.** When you're ready to bake, put the risen loaf (on its tray) into the oven and pour about 100ml of cold water into the hot roasting tin in the bottom of the oven and shut the oven door. The burst of steam will help form a crisp crust on the loaf.

7 Immediately lower the oven temperature to 220°C/200°C fan/ Gas 7. Bake the loaf for 30–35 minutes, until golden. To test whether or not the loaf is fully baked, tap the underside. It should be firm and sound hollow. Transfer the loaf to a wire rack and leave it to cool completely before slicing and eating.

Sausage rolls

Makes: 6
Hands on: 45 mins + resting
Bake: 35 mins

FOR THE CHEAT'S ROUGH PUFF
240g plain flour,
    plus extra for dusting
pinch of salt
40g unsalted butter,
    chilled and cut into cubes
100g unsalted butter, frozen
1 egg, beaten, to glaze

FOR THE FILLING
475g pork sausagemeat
1 tsp dried sage
2 tsp Dijon mustard
sea salt and freshly ground
    black pepper

You will need
baking sheet, lined
    with baking paper

There are so many options for the definitive pastry recipe, but, here at *Bake Off*, we do love a sausage roll. We have the ancient Romans to thank for the idea of wrapping meat in dough, although it's likely that the sausage roll as we know it was dreamed up in 19th-century France.

· · · · · · · · · · · ·

1 **Make the cheat's rough puff.** Mix the flour and salt together in a bowl. Rub in the chilled butter using your fingertips until the mixture resembles breadcrumbs. Little by little, add enough water to form a dough (you'll need about 4–6 tablespoons).

2 Lightly flour your work surface and roll out the dough into a rectangle, about 45 x 15cm.

3 Coarsely grate half of the frozen butter over the bottom two thirds of the dough. Fold down the top third and fold up the bottom third as if folding a letter.

4 Turn the folded dough through 90 degrees and roll it out into a rectangle again. Repeat the process of adding the remaining frozen butter and fold as before. Wrap the dough in cling film and leave to rest in the fridge for 30 minutes.

5 **Make the filling.** Mix the sausagemeat and sage together, then season with salt and pepper. Divide the mixture into six equal portions and shape each into a cylinder, about 10cm long. Place the sausage cylinders on a baking sheet lined with baking paper and chill them in the fridge.

6 Heat the oven to 200°C/180°C fan/Gas 6.

7 **Assemble the sausage rolls.** Place the chilled pastry on a lightly floured work surface and roll it out to a square that measures about 30 x 30cm. Cut it into six equal rectangles, each measuring 10 x 15cm.

8 Spread each rectangle of pastry with Dijon mustard. Place the sausagemeat cylinders just above centre, horizontally across the width of each rectangle of pastry. Pick up one short end of each rectangle and fold it over the filling to meet the other short end, sealing the edges together. Crimp with a fork so you have a visible seam running along the side of each sausage roll.

9 **Finish the sausage rolls.** Place the sausage rolls on the lined baking sheet and glaze them with the beaten egg. Bake for 30–35 minutes, until the pastry is golden-brown and the sausagemeat is cooked through.

PATISSERIE
Chocolate éclairs

It's said that in the 19th century, French chef Marie-Antoine Carême experimented by filling a long choux bun with cream, and topping it with chocolate – and so, the story goes, this most famous of pâtissérie delights was born.

. . . .

Makes: 18
Hands on: 45 mins
Bake: 50 mins

FOR THE CRÈME PÂTISSIÈRE
300ml whole milk
150ml double cream
3 large egg yolks
1 tsp vanilla extract
50g caster sugar
50g cornflour

FOR THE CHOUX
110g unsalted butter
180g plain flour
4 large eggs, beaten

FOR THE CHOCOLATE ICING
3 tbsp cocoa powder
200g icing sugar

You will need
baking sheet, lined with
    baking paper
large piping bag fitted with
    a 1.25cm plain nozzle
medium piping bag fitted
    with a small plain nozzle

1 **Make the crème pâtissière.** Heat the milk and cream together in a pan on a low heat until simmering.

2 Meanwhile, in a separate bowl whisk together the egg yolks, vanilla, caster sugar and cornflour, then pour the hot milk mixture over, whisking continuously until smooth.

3 Return the mixture to the pan, then whisk it over a low heat until thickened. Pour the crème pâtissière onto a large baking tray and cover it with cling film. Leave to cool completely.

4 **Make the choux buns.** Pour 260ml of water into a pan and add the butter. Bring to the boil on a medium heat and stir to combine. Add the flour, then remove the pan from the heat and beat the mixture vigorously with a wooden spoon until it comes away from the sides of the pan. Spread the mixture over a plate and leave it to cool for 15 minutes.

5 Meanwhile, heat the oven to 200°C/180°C fan/Gas 6. Draw 18 lines, each 10cm long, on the paper lining your baking sheet. Turn the baking paper drawn-side down.

6 Return the choux mixture to a bowl and, a little at a time, add the beaten eggs, until you reach a dropping consistency (the mixture will fall easily from the spoon in a blob).

7 Spoon the choux mixture into the large piping bag with the 1.25cm nozzle. Pipe 18 lines of choux on the lined baking sheet, using the pencil lines as a guide. Flatten any pointed ends with a damp finger. Bake for 40 minutes, until puffed and golden.

8 Skewer a hole in the end of each bun to allow the steam to escape and return them to the oven for a further 5 minutes, then remove them from the oven and transfer them to a wire rack to cool completely.

9 **Make the icing.** While the buns are cooling, put the icing ingredients in a bowl, then add enough water, a little at a time, until the icing is glossy and firm.

10 **Assemble the buns.** Spoon the crème pâtissière into the medium piping bag with the small nozzle. Insert the end of the nozzle into the steam hole in each bun and fill each with equal amounts of the crème. Use a spoon to spread icing over each bun and allow it to set.

Apple plate pie

Serves: 6
Hands on: 30 mins + chilling
Bake: 35 mins

275g plain flour
2 tbsp icing sugar
140g unsalted butter,
    chilled and diced
3–4 tbsp chilled water
1 egg, beaten
2 tsp caster sugar,
    for sprinkling

FOR THE FILLING
2 large cooking apples
    (about 700g), peeled,
    cored and sliced
4 tbsp caster sugar
1 cinnamon stick
2 tbsp semolina
2 eating apples, peeled,
    cored and thinly sliced

You will need
24cm pie plate

While the Americans may claim this classic dessert as their own (you've heard the phrase 'as American as apple pie'), in fact there are references to a pie made with apples (and other fruit) in 14th-century English texts, and Dutch recipes for apple pie date back to the 1400s. This one is made in the traditional way – in a pie plate with a full crust.

. . . .

1 **Make the pastry.** Put the flour and icing sugar in a large bowl and mix to combine. Add the butter and use your fingertips to rub it in until the mixture resembles fine breadcrumbs. A couple of teaspoons at a time, add the water, mixing between each addition, until you've added just enough to bring the pastry together. Gently knead the pastry into a ball, then wrap it in cling film and chill for 30 minutes to rest.

2 **Make the filling.** Place the cooking apple slices in a pan along with the caster sugar, cinnamon stick and 3 tablespoons of water. Cook, stirring occasionally, on a medium heat, until the apples begin to collapse, but still hold their shape. Transfer the apples to a clean bowl, discarding the cinnamon stick, and leave to cool.

3 Heat the oven to 200°C/180°C fan/Gas 6.

4 **Assemble the pie.** Remove the pastry from the fridge and divide it into two unequal pieces, roughly ⅔ and ⅓. Place the larger piece on a lightly floured work surface and roll it out to 2–3mm thick. Use this pastry sheet to line the base of the pie plate. Then, roll out the smaller pastry piece to 2–3mm thick to form the pie lid.

5 Sprinkle the semolina over the pastry base. Mix the sliced eating apples with the cooled apple filling and tip the apple mixture onto the pie base, spreading it out evenly, but leaving a ring of pastry around the edge.

6 Brush the edges of the pie with beaten egg, then cover the filling with the lid. Crimp the edges using the tines of a fork to press down on the pastry rim, then trim away any excess. Use any pastry trimmings to make decorations for the top, if you wish.

7 Brush the top of the pie with more beaten egg, then sprinkle with the 2 teaspoons of caster sugar. Make three small slits in the top of the pie to let the steam out.

8 Bake the pie for 30–35 minutes, until golden brown. Remove it from the oven and leave it to rest for 15 minutes before serving. Enjoy with ice cream, cream or custard.

CHOCOLATE

Chocolate fondants

Makes: 4
Hands on: 20 mins
Bake: 10 mins

2 tbsp cocoa powder, for dusting
110g 70% dark chocolate, chopped
110g unsalted butter
2 eggs
2 egg yolks
55g caster sugar
2 tbsp plain flour

You will need
175ml pudding moulds x 4,
　　thoroughly and evenly
　　greased with butter

Remarkably, the classic chocolate fondant dessert may be barely 40 years old, having been patented in the early 1980s by a Michelin-starred French chef (although it could have been cooked up by an American housewife in the 1960s – the debate goes on). Either way, despite its relative youth, the fondant now defines chocolate-pudding heaven.

. . . .

1　Heat the oven to 200°C/180°C fan/Gas 6. Dust the insides of the greased moulds with the cocoa powder, tapping out any excess. Place the dusted moulds in the freezer while you make the batter.

2　**Make the fondant batter.** Melt the dark chocolate and butter together in a bowl set over a pan of barely simmering water. Stir until melted, then remove the bowl from the heat and leave the chocolate mixture to cool.

3　Whisk the eggs, egg yolks and caster sugar together in a large bowl, until it becomes thick and mousse-like, and leaves a ribbon trail when you lift the whisk.

4　Carefully fold the cooled, melted chocolate mixture into the egg mixture. Then, sift the flour over the top and fold it in using a spoon, taking care not to knock out any air. Divide the mixture equally between the four prepared moulds.

5　**Bake the fondants.** Place the filled pudding moulds on a baking tray and into the oven. Bake the fondants for 10 minutes, until they are risen but not cracked. They should still have a slight wobble. Turn out the fondants and serve immediately.

224 ORIGINAL KITCHEN CLASSICS

Vegan meringue kisses

The word 'aquafaba' – the name given to the water you'll find in a can of chickpeas – is a modern nomenclature derived from the Latin words for water (*aqua*) and bean (*faba*). As we look for ways to eat a more plant-based diet, aquafaba offers a good alternative to egg white for making these perfect little meringue kisses.

Makes: 40
Hands on: 45 mins
Bake: 2 hours

125ml aquafaba
½ tsp xanthan gum
270g caster sugar
1 tbsp lemon juice
1 tsp cornflour

You will need
large piping bag
2 baking sheets, lined
   with baking paper

. . . .

1 Heat the oven to 80°C/Gas ¼ (don't use the fan oven).

2 Put the aquafaba and xanthan gum in the bowl of a stand mixer fitted with the whisk. Whisk the mixture on high speed until it forms stiff peaks.

3 With the whisk still running, gradually add the caster sugar, one spoonful at a time, whisking until the mixture is thick and glossy. Add the lemon juice and cornflour and whisk again to combine.

4 Spoon the meringue into the piping bag and snip the end to make a 1cm hole. Pipe 20 meringue kisses onto each lined baking sheet.

5 Bake for 1½–2 hours, until firm. Remove the meringue kisses from the oven and leave them to cool. Serve immediately.

Baking Tips

Folding in
This is a way to combine ingredients gently so you don't knock out all the air, ideally with a large metal spoon or rubber spatula. Cut down through the mixture to the bottom of the bowl, turn the spoon or spatula and draw it up, then flip it over so the mixture flops onto the surface. Give the bowl a quarter turn and repeat.

Rubbing in
This is a way to combine butter and flour and add air when making pastry and simple cake mixtures. Pick up a little butter and flour mixture in your fingers and thumbs (cooler than your palms), lift and gently rub your fingers and thumbs together to combine the mixture as it falls. Keep doing this until the mixture has a crumb-like consistency.

Blind baking
Line the pastry case with the baking paper (cut to size and crumpled up to make it more flexible) and fill with ceramic baking beans, rice or dried beans. Bake as stated in the recipe (or for about 12–15 minutes, until set and firm). Remove the paper and beans, then return the pastry case to the oven and bake for a further 5–10 minutes, until the pastry is thoroughly cooked and starting to colour.

Homemade jam
For about 425g of jam (a standard jar), you'll need about 250g fruit and 250g jam sugar. Tip the fruit into a large, heavy-based pan, add the sugar and gently squash the fruit with a potato masher or the back of a wooden spoon, keeping a bit of texture. Stir the fruit gently over a low heat with a wooden spoon until the sugar dissolves. Increase the heat and boil rapidly, stirring to prevent the jam catching, until the jam reaches 105°C on a sugar thermometer. Pour the jam into a warm, sterilised jar, place a wax disc on top and leave to cool completely. Cover with a sterilised lid. Use within 1 month.

Breadmaking Tips

Kneading bread dough
Kneading develops the gluten in the flour to create a structure that stretches around the bubbles of carbon dioxide released as the yeast (or other raising agent) activates in the heat of the oven. To knead by hand, turn out the dough onto a lightly floured or oiled worktop. Hold one end with your hand and use the other hand to pull and stretch out the dough away from you. Gather the dough back into a ball again, give it a quarter turn, then repeat the stretching and gathering. As you knead, the dough starts to feel pliable, then stretchy, then very elastic and silky. Nearly all doughs need 10 minutes hand kneading. In a stand mixer, use a dough hook on the lowest speed and knead for about 5 minutes. While it's almost impossible to over-knead by hand, you can stretch the gluten too much in a mixer, which can hamper the rise. To test if the dough has been kneaded enough, stretch a small piece between your fingers to a thin, translucent sheet. If it won't stretch or it tears easily, knead it for longer.

Rising and proving
Place the dough in a moist, warm spot. A room temperature of 20–24°C is ideal – if the room is too hot, the yeast will grow too rapidly and the dough will become distorted (and maybe develop a slight aftertaste); too cool and the yeast develops more slowly (although this can give a richer flavour and chewier crumb). Proving is the last period of rising prior to baking, after shaping a bread dough. To test whether the dough is well proved, gently prod it: if it springs back, it's not ready; if it returns to its original state fairly slowly, or if there's a very slight dent left, it's ready.

Knocking back bread dough

Knocking back or punching down risen dough happens after rising and before shaping and proving. It breaks up the large gas bubbles to make smaller, finer bubbles that expand more evenly during baking, causing a more even rise. Use your knuckles to punch down the dough. Some bakers fold or flop the dough over on itself a few times.

Perfecting a bread crust

Make sure the oven is thoroughly heated, so the dough quickly puffs (called 'oven-spring') and then sets evenly. For a crisp upper crust, create a burst of steam to keep the surface of the bread moist. To create the steam, put an empty roasting tin on the floor of the oven as it heats up. Then, immediately as you put in the unbaked loaf, pour cold water or throw a handful of ice cubes into the hot tin. Close the door to trap in the steam. For a crisp base, put a baking sheet or baking stone in the oven to heat up. Then carefully transfer your loaf onto the hot baking sheet or stone for baking.

Sourdough starter

Making a starter can take from 6 days to 2 weeks, depending on which flour you use and the ambient temperature of your kitchen. You'll need 150g organic white bread flour and 150g organic rye or spelt flour, and lukewarm (never hot) water, as well as an airtight box.

Day 1 Combine the flours and store in an airtight box or jar. Mix 25g of the flour mixture with 25ml cool water in a glass or ceramic bowl and beat to a smooth paste. Cover the bowl loosely with baking paper, securing it with a rubber band, and leave it for 24 hours at room temperature. Total weight = 50g.

Day 2 Mix 25g of the flour mixture with 25ml lukewarm water to a paste and combine it with the Day One starter. Cover again and set aside for 24 hours. Total weight = 100g.

Day 3 Discard half the mixture (50g). Add 25g of the flour mixture and 25ml lukewarm water to the remaining starter. Scoop into a glass jar. Cover loosely with the lid and set aside for 24 hours. Total weight = 100g.

Day 4 Repeat day 3. Total weight = 100g.

Day 5 Mix 100g of the flour mixture and 100ml lukewarm water to a paste and add this to the starter. Combine thoroughly, then cover loosely with the lid and leave for 24 hours. Total weight = 300g.

Day 6 Discard half the starter and add 75g of the flour mixture and 75ml water. Total weight = 300g.

Your starter should be bubbly and active and have a fresh, yeasty smell. Repeat this process for another 6 days, remembering to keep the ratio of flour to water the same at every feed. If the starter is slow after 6 days, feed it twice a day, each feed 12 hours apart. Once active, store your starter in the fridge between uses. Bring it back to room temperature and feed it the day before using it again.

A Baker's Kitchen

You don't need a lot to be able to bake. With an oven, scales, a bowl and a baking sheet you can bake bread, biscuits, scones... add a couple of cake tins and a wooden spoon and you can whip up a cake. So, although the following list seems long, please don't feel overwhelmed – build up your kitchen gradually, as you build up your skills.

Baking beans

An essential to keep the base of a pastry case flat and the side upright while you blind bake (that is, bake it without its filling). Ceramic baking beans intended for this purpose are handy and reusable, but uncooked dried beans, lentils or rice will work well multiple times, too. Just make sure you store them in a labelled jar afterwards as, once baked, they won't be suitable for eating.

Baking paper and liners

These help prevent sticking. Choose non-stick baking paper (sometimes called parchment). Greaseproof is less sturdy and has a waxy coating that doesn't stand up as well to the heat of the oven. Reusable silicone liners are more expensive, but are easy to use, can be cut to fit your tins and trays (or buy them ready-cut) and can be wiped clean. With proper care they can last for life.

Baking sheets and trays

A baking sheet is flat with only one raised edge for gripping, making it good for bakes (such as biscuits and pavlovas) that you might want to slide to another surface. A baking tray has a rim or shallow edge all the way around. Aim to have at least one heavy-duty baking sheet, and two or three trays or lightweight sheets.

Baking tins

Always use the baking tin that's specified in the recipe as the quantities and baking time have been calculated accordingly. (See the 'You Will Need' lists at the end of each set of ingredients.) A really solid, good-quality tin will withstand repeated baking without scorching or losing its shape. Clean and dry your tins thoroughly after you've used them. Occasionally, a recipe will call for a specialist tin or mould, but in general the following will see you through nicely:

Loaf tins are essential for neat, brick-shaped breads and cakes. They're available in a variety of sizes, but the most-used sizes are 450g (measuring about 19 x 12.5 x 7.5cm and also sold as 1lb loaf tins) and 900g (measuring about 26 x 12.5 x 7.5cm, and also sold as 2lb loaf tins). Heavy-duty loaf tins won't dent or warp and will give you a better crust than equivalent silicone versions.

Muffin or cupcake tins are what you need for small bakes. They are usually 6- or 12-hole. Non-stick and silicone versions will produce equally good results, so choose what suits you best.

Pudding moulds (mini ones) are a bit of a luxury, but handy for making individual dessert bakes, such as individual chocolate fondants and sponge puddings.

Sandwich (or sponge) tins are essential. Aim to own two 20cm-diameter sandwich or round cake tins, each 4–5cm deep. A third tin is useful for baking American-style layer cakes.

Springform (or springclip) tins are deep metal tins with a spring release. Use them for cakes, tortes, pies, cheesecakes and pull-apart bread rolls because they won't damage the side of a fragile bake as you remove it.

Swiss roll tins are rectangular (usually 20 x 30cm or 23 x 33cm) and about 2cm deep.

Tart and tartlet tins, available with fluted and straight sides, give the most professional results when made from sturdy metal, such as anodised aluminium. Choose non-stick, loose-bottomed versions for the best results. ***Traybake*** tins are square or rectangular and about 4cm deep, and are used for brownies, shortbread and all traybakes. Buy loose-bottomed tins to help free your bakes easily.

Bowls

For versatility, sturdiness and durability, heatproof glass and stainless steel bowls are good choices for mixing and whisking, and glass or ceramic are best for melting ingredients over hot water, although plastic bowls are cheaper. (Note, too, that ceramic bowls look pretty but can be heavy.) A very large bowl with a snap-on lid is useful for mixing and rising bread doughs. Incidentally, make your bowls non-slip by resting them on a damp cloth as you mix.

Cake-decorating turntable

A cake-decorating turntable makes easy work of smoothing out buttercreams or ganache around the sides of a cake. It's especially handy if you're going for a semi-naked effect (such as in the Vegan Coffee and Walnut Cake on page 198) or perhaps an ombre effect.

Cooling/wire racks

A large wire rack with legs allows air to circulate around and underneath a bake as it cools, avoiding any sogginess. A clean wire grill-pan rack makes a good improvisation, if necessary.

Dough scraper

One of the cheapest and most useful pieces of equipment, the dough scraper helps to scoop, scrape and divide bread dough, and makes easy work of cleaning bowls and worktops.

Electric stand mixers, processors and whisks

Lots of the recipes in the book call for a helping hand from an electric gadget, such as a stand mixer. Although these can make life easier, if you're new to baking, don't feel you have to rush out and buy one. Most of the recipes in the book can be made with muscle power – just remember to keep going (with a hand whisk, a wooden spoon, or your bare hands), until you reach the consistency described in the method.

A large-capacity stand mixer is a good investment if you do a lot of baking. Use the whisk attachment for meringues, buttercreams and light sponge mixtures; the paddle or beater attachment for heavier mixtures, such as richer cakes, choux pastry, and savarin-type enriched doughs; and the dough hook for mixing, then kneading bread doughs. A spare bowl will help with multi-element sponges.

An electric hand whisk is a good, versatile choice if you want to make whisked mixtures, creamed sponges, meringues, buttercreams or batter, or mixtures whisked over heat.

A hand-held stick blender (often with a whisk attachment, too) is good for smoothing out fruit sauces and crème pâtissière.

A food processor makes light work of blending fat and flour to make pastry. Use the 'pulse' button to avoid any overworking. It's also good for finely chopping nuts and herbs (try a mini version for small quantities).

Hand or balloon whisk

A wire hand whisk can be balloon-shaped or flat; a hand-held rotary whisk consists of a pair of beaters in a metal frame. Any of these is essential, even if you have an electric version.

Knives

The better the knife, the better your knife skills. Stainless steel knives are easy to keep clean, but need to be sharpened regularly; carbon-steel knives are more expensive, but easier to keep sharp. Gather a medium knife, about 20cm long; a small knife (useful for pastry work, trimming edges, and making decorations); and a good-quality serrated bread knife (for sawing through crusts).

Lame

A lame is useful for scoring bread – it's like a double-sided razor blade on a handle.

Measuring equipment

Baking is a science and, for perfect results, precision is essential. The following pieces of measuring equipment are must-haves for guaranteed success.

Digital scales are particularly useful. As well as weighing tiny ingredients and switching easily between units, you can 'zero' ingredients you've already weighed, then add further ingredients to the same bowl, weighing each as you go.

Measuring jugs, even if you have digital scales, are a must. Pick a heat-resistant and microwave-safe jug that starts at 50ml (ideally) or 100ml, and goes up to 2 litres.

Measuring spoons do a far better job than everyday spoons (teaspoons, dessert spoons, tablespoons), which will give inconsistent results. Spoon measures in this book are level, not heaped or rounded, unless specified.

Metal spoon

A large, long metal spoon is invaluable for folding wet ingredients into dry.

Oven thermometer

Built-in oven thermostats can be inconsistent between brands and will become less efficient with age, so an oven thermometer is a good way to make sure your oven reaches the right temperature before you bake, as well as to identify the hot and cool spots to avoid uneven bakes. If you don't have a thermometer, get to know your oven, then increase or decrease the temperature or baking time accordingly to get the right results.

Palette knife

An offset palette knife (with a kink near the handle) is useful for spreading icings and delicate mixtures where you need a smooth, precise result. A straight palette knife is good for lifting and moving bakes from one surface to another.

Pastry brush

Opt for a heat- and dishwasher-proof, medium pastry brush – essential both for glazing pastry and bread and for brushing down sugar crystals in a pan as you make caramel.

Pastry cutters

Pick a double-sided (plain on one side, fluted on the other) nest of metal cutters. A pizza wheel-cutter is handy for cutting straight lines. Shaped cutters are infinite and lovely, too.

Piping bags and nozzles

The recipes in this book use both reusable and paper piping bags in various sizes. Piping nozzles range from wide, round tips for piping choux pastry and meringue, to star-shaped for icings, to small writing tips for delicate work. Set the nozzle in the bag, stand it in a jug, tall glass or a mug for support, then fill. Twist the top before you pipe to stop the contents of the bag escaping the wrong way. To keep things simple, we use small, medium and large when referring to the size of piping nozzles. As a guide, a small piping nozzle is about 5mm in diameter (a size 1 or 2 writing nozzle); a medium nozzle, about 1cm; and a large nozzle, about 1.5cm. An open star nozzle gives less distinct peaks and troughs in the piping (as in an iced gem) than a closed star nozzle.

Proving bags

Although not strictly necessary (covering with oiled cling film will do), proving bags (ideally two) are reusable, which makes them kinder to the environment. Lightly oil the inside of the bag, then slide in your dough on a baking tray and inflate the bag a little to stop the dough sticking to it as it rises.

Rolling pin

A fairly heavy wooden pin about 6–7cm in diameter and without handles will make the easiest work of rolling out pastry.

Rubber spatula

A strong and flexible spatula is useful for mixing, folding and scraping with ease.

Sieve

Every baker needs a sieve – to combine flour with raising agents; remove lumps from icing and sugars; and for straining and puréeing. Go for a large metal sieve that will sit over your largest bowl for sifting tasks, and a smaller, tea-strainer-sized one for dusting.

Sugar thermometer/Cooking thermometer

Essential for sugar work (and deep-frying), a sugar thermometer will ensure your sugar reaches the correct temperature if, for example, you're making caramel or nougat, or tempering chocolate – among other baking tasks. Pick one that's easy to read and can clip onto the side of the pan. A thermometer with a probe will help you to measure the internal temperatures of your bakes for doneness, too.

Timer

A digital kitchen timer with seconds as well as minutes (and a loud bell) is essential baking equipment – don't rely on just your oven timer. Set the timer for a minute or two less than the suggested time in your recipe (especially if you're uncertain of your oven) – you can always increase the time your bake is in the oven if it's not quite done yet.

Wooden spoon

Cheap, heat-resistant, and safe on non-stick pans, a wooden spoon mixes, beats, creams and stirs – the essentials of good baking. (You can even use the handle to shape brandy snaps and tuiles.) Store your savoury and sweet spoons separately, as wood can absorb strong flavours.

Zester

A long-handled zester is the best and quickest way to remove the zest from citrus fruits (use unwaxed citrus fruits for zesting). Pick one that's sturdy and easy to hold.

A Baker's Larder

Most of the bakes in this book use ingredients that are easy to find and store. Keep the following in your cupboard and, whether you need to whip up something for a cake sale, find an activity for the kids, or create a dinner-party showstopper, you'll be ready to start baking. As a rule of thumb: the best-quality ingredients tend to give the best results.

Baking powder, bicarbonate of soda and cream of tartar

Chemical raising agents, all these ingredients increase the lightness and volume of cakes and small bakes, and some types of biscuit and pastry. Always use the amount given in the recipe – but check the date stamps before you start, as raising agents will lose their potency over time. If you've run out of baking powder, you can easily make your own: for 1 teaspoon of baking powder combine ½ teaspoon of cream of tartar with ¼ teaspoon of bicarbonate of soda. If you are making a gluten-free bake, bear in mind that baking powder should be gluten-free, but some manufacturers add filling agents that may contain gluten. Always check the label.

Butter and other fats

Most of the recipes in this book use unsalted butter, as it has a delicate flavour, adds a good, even colour (perhaps because it contains less whey than salted), and allows you to season your bake to taste yourself, as relevant. Store butter tightly wrapped in the fridge, well away from strong flavours. When relevant, a recipe will tell you whether to use butter chilled (from the fridge) or softened at room temperature (in that case, don't be tempted to soften it in the microwave – you're looking for a texture that yields easily when pressed with a finger, but holds the shape, not melted). Cubed butter enables you to add small amounts at a time and makes the butter easier to combine with the other ingredients.

Dairy-free spreads, made from vegetable and sunflower oils, make good substitutes in most recipes that require softened or room-temperature butter, but always check the label to make sure it's good for baking beforehand. Some are made specifically for baking and you can use them straight from the fridge. They give good results, but may lack that buttery flavour. Avoid spreads designed for use on bread/crackers – they contain too much water and not enough fat to make good baking ingredients.

Lard, from pigs, gives a short, flaky texture to traditional hot-water-crust pastry so that it bakes to a crisp, golden finish. White solid vegetable fat is a good alternative.

Oil often pops up in bakes these days. Vegetable oil is a good all-rounder, but in baking, sunflower oil gives the best results as it's especially light and mildly flavoured.

Solid coconut oil is a good option for dairy-free and vegan recipes, but isn't a like-for-like butter substitute.

Suet, from cows in its non-vegetarian form, gives a light, soft pastry rather than a very crisp or flaky one. Suet is more solid than butter or lard and melts much more slowly, forming tiny pockets in the dough as it cooks. Most supermarkets sell vegetarian suet, too.

Chocolate

Chocolate is a must in baking – from shards and shavings to ganache and buttercream, it features in many of the recipes in this book. Dark chocolate, with around 54% cocoa solids, is the kind most used in these recipes as it gives a good balance of flavour. Some recipes recommend 70% dark, which is a little less sweet. Chocolate with a higher percentage (75% and above) may be too bitter and dry for general baking. Milk chocolate has a much milder and sweeter flavour – choose a good-quality favourite, and expect the best results from milk chocolate with good amounts of cocoa solids. White chocolate doesn't contain any cocoa solids, just cocoa butter. Look out for brands with 30% or more cocoa butter as a measure of quality. White chocolate sets less firmly than dark or milk chocolate owing to the higher fat content, and melts at a lower temperature, so take care as it easily scorches and so will become unusable.

Cocoa powder

A dark, unsweetened powder made from pure, dried cocoa beans, once the cocoa butter has been removed. Cocoa powder is very bitter, strongly flavoured and gives a powerful hit. Never substitute cocoa powder with drinking chocolate, which contains milk powder and sugar, as well as cocoa powder itself.

Cream

Chill cream thoroughly before whipping (in hot weather, also chill the bowl and whisk). *Buttermilk,* sometimes labelled 'cultured buttermilk', is low-fat or non-fat milk plus a bacterial culture to give it an acidic tang. It is often used along with bicarbonate of soda to add lightness as well as flavour to scones and cakes.
Crème fraîche is a soured cream with a creamy, tangy flavour. It won't whip, but you can use it for fillings, toppings and serving.
Double cream contains at least 48% butterfat. It whips well and has a richer flavour than whipping cream. The extra-rich type of double cream available is designed for spooning, rather than for whipping or ganache.
Lactose-free and soy-based dairy-free creams can give varied results, and are usually unsuitable for whipping.
Single cream contains 18% butterfat and is good for adding to sauces and fillings, for adding richness to rubbed-in mixtures, or for pouring over desserts and pastries.

Soured cream has only 18% butterfat. It is made by introducing a bacterial culture to cream, giving a naturally sour tang.
Whipping cream usually contains at least 36% butterfat and is designed to whip well without being overly rich.

Dried fruit

Store dried fruit out of direct sunlight and sealed in containers. Vine fruit, such as raisins, sultanas and currants, have a long shelf-life, but are best bought when you need them. Soft-dried apricots, as well as dried figs, cranberries, blueberries, sour cherries, and dates, can replace vine fruits in many recipes. They add sweetness and moisture, which is useful if you want to reduce refined sugar.

Eggs

When it comes to eggs, size really does matter. Unless otherwise stated, all the recipes in this book use medium eggs. If the eggs are too small, a sponge may not rise properly and look thin or dry; too big and a pastry or bread dough may be too wet or soft to handle.
For baking, use eggs at room temperature, which means taking them out of the fridge 30–60 minutes before you start cooking. If you forget, pop them into a bowl of lukewarm water for a couple of minutes.
Spare egg whites will keep for 3–4 days in a sealed container or jar in the fridge, or for up to a month in the freezer (defrost them overnight in the fridge before using; note that egg yolks can't be frozen).

Extracts and flavourings

Avoid synthetic flavourings as much as you can – they often have an aftertaste that will spoil your hard work balancing your flavours. Here's a guide to the best to use.
Almond extract may be pricey, but most recipes need only a few drops. Avoid anything marked 'flavouring'.

Ground spices are best when you use them fresh, but if you're storing them, do so in screw-topped jars, rather than open packets.
Vanilla is usually the most expensive flavouring used in baking, although you need only small amounts. Vanilla extract – labelled 'pure' or 'natural' – costs more than vanilla essence, which might contain artificial flavourings. Vanilla paste is made from the seeds of the pods and has a thicker texture and more concentrated flavour. Best of all, though, are vanilla pods, which you can split to scrape out the tiny seeds to flavour custards and fillings. Don't throw away the pods: rinse and dry them, then put them in a jar of caster sugar to make vanilla sugar.

Flour

Whether made from wheat or other grains, flour has to be the most valued ingredient in the baker's larder. Avoid poor-quality, out-of-date or stale flour, as this will affect the result and taste of the final bake. Always buy the best and freshest flour you can afford.
Cornflour is added to biscuits to give a delicate crumb, and used to thicken custard and crème pâtissière.
Gluten-free flours are wheat-free mixtures of several ingredients, including rice, potato, tapioca, maize, chickpea, broad bean, white sorghum or buckwheat – depending on the brand. Ready-mixed gluten-free flours sometimes suggest adding xanthan gum (a powder sold in small tubs) to improve the texture and crumb of your bake – check the packet and, if your flour mixture doesn't already include it, add 1 teaspoon of xanthan gum per 150g gluten-free flour. Some gluten-free flours need a little more liquid than wheat flour doughs, so you can't substitute them exactly, but it is well worth experimenting.
Plain flour is a type of wheat flour used for making pastry, pancakes and rich fruit cakes, for example, and has no added raising agents.

Rye flour has a deep, dark flavour that works well in breads, particularly sourdoughs. It's low in gluten, which makes it harder to knead than wheat flours, and the dough rises less well. Available as wholegrain and a finer 'light' rye, which has had some of the bran sifted out, it is useful for crackers and adding to wheat flour for savoury pastry recipes.
Self-raising flour has added baking powder and gives a light, risen texture to sponges. If you run out of self-raising flour you can make your own: add 4 teaspoons of baking powder to every 225g plain flour, sifting them together a couple of times. Sponge self-raising flour is more expensive than regular self-raising, but is slightly 'softer' and silkier.
Semolina flour is a slightly gritty, pale yellow flour made from durum wheat, and is often used for pasta and Italian-style breads (as well as semolina pudding).
Speciality wheat flours are created from wheat varieties that are specifically grown to make flour for baking ciabatta, pizza bases, and baguettes.
Spelt flour comes from the same family as wheat, but has a slightly different genetic make-up and a richer and more nutty flavour – it is good for most recipes that call for flour, except very delicate biscuits and sponges.
Stoneground flour means that the grain (wheat, rye, spelt and so on) is milled between large stones instead of steel rollers, giving a coarser texture and fuller flavour.
Strong bread flour is made from wheat with a higher ratio of protein to starch than the cake and pastry flours. This increased ratio is crucial to bread-making: as you knead the dough, the protein develops into strands of gluten that stretch as the gases produced by the yeast expand, enabling the dough to rise. Strong bread flour has about 12–16% protein, which is ideal for most breads. Extra-strong or Canadian strong flour has even more (15–17%) – good for bagels or larger loaves.

Wholemeal or wholegrain flours are made from the complete wheat kernel, making them far more nutritious than white flours (which are made using 75% of the cleaned wheat kernel, and have most of the wheat bran and wheatgerm removed). The small specks of bran in these flours mean that they give a dough that rises less well than one made with all white flour. Wholemeal plain flour has been milled to make it lighter and more suitable for making pastry and cakes.

Nuts

Buy nuts in small quantities to use up quickly (always before the use-by date) – the high oil content means that once opened, nuts can quickly turn rancid. If you're storing them, do so in an airtight container in a cool, dark place. Most nuts benefit from being lightly toasted before use, to impart a richer, nuttier flavour to the finished bake.

Almonds are incredibly versatile – ground, chopped, flaked (toasted and untoasted) and whole (blanched or unblanched). To blanch (remove the skins) yourself, put the nuts in a small pan, add water to cover and bring to the boil. Remove the pan from the heat and drain, then slip the nuts out of their casings. Dry on kitchen paper.

Hazelnuts are usually ready-blanched (without their brown papery skins) or ground.

Pistachios are easy to find shelled and unsalted, but they usually come with their papery skins attached. To reveal the deep-green colour of the nuts, carefully tip them into a pan of boiling water. Remove from the heat, leave for 1 minute, then drain. Transfer the nuts to a clean, dry tea towel and rub gently to loosen the skins, then peel if necessary. Ready-ground pistachios are also available these days.

Walnuts and pecans, usually halved or chopped, are interchangeable in most baking recipes as they share a similar texture and appearance (walnuts are slightly more bitter). Gently toasting walnuts and pecans in a medium-heat oven gives them a much deeper, richer flavour.

Sugar

Different sugars combine and interact with other ingredients in different ways, affecting the end results of the bake. Always use the sugar the recipe specifies. Sugar doesn't have a shelf-life and will keep indefinitely in an airtight container in a cool, dark place.

Caster sugar comes as both refined white and unrefined golden. White provides sweetness with a neutral colour and flavour that is, for example, perfect for white meringues or very pale sponges. Unrefined golden caster sugar has a slight caramel, rich flavour. Use it when a warmer colour in your bake is not an issue. The fine grains of caster sugar break down easily during beating or creaming with butter for sponges, melt quickly for lemon curd, and disappear in pastry.

Fondant icing sugar sets hard, so it's good for decorating as it doesn't smudge. It contains glucose syrup to give a smooth, glossy finish.

Granulated sugar, available as white or golden, has bigger grains that take longer to dissolve. Keep it for making sugar syrups and drizzles, and for sprinkling on top of bakes to give a satisfying crunch.

Icing sugar is also available as refined (white) and unrefined (golden). Again, the unrefined version has a pale caramel colour and flavour. Use white icing sugar for icings, fillings and frostings that need to be very pale or that are to be coloured with food colouring. Sift icing sugar before use to remove any lumps so that your icing is perfectly smooth.

Jam sugar contains added pectin to help jam set, making it good for making jams that use fruits without high natural levels of pectin – raspberries, strawberries, apricots and ripe cherries, among them.

Muscovado sugars come as light muscovado and dark muscovado. These add a stronger, warmer caramel or molasses flavour and darker colour to bakes, but they can make them more moist and heavy. They are good in rich fruity cakes, gingerbreads, parkins, and spice cakes. Press out any lumps with the back of a spoon before using.

Syrup and treacle

Golden syrup and thick black treacle add a rich, toffee-ish flavour, as well as sweetness, to bakes. They can be difficult to measure if you're spooning out of a tin, so warm the measuring spoon in a mug of just-boiled water before scooping, or stand the syrup or treacle tin in a bowl of boiled water for a few minutes to loosen the stickiness. Easier is to use a squeezy bottle – many brands of golden syrup now come readily available this way (similarly, for honey). Maple syrup has a lighter texture than golden syrup, but a distinctive flavour that works particularly well with nuts, and, of course, over pancakes.

Yeast

Yeast is a living organism that makes bread doughs rise. It needs moisture, gentle warmth and flour (or sugar) to stimulate its growth and the production of carbon dioxide, which expands the dough. Some recipes use fast-action dried yeast, available in 7g sachets or in tubs as easy blend or instant dried yeast. Always weigh your yeast, unless it's the exact amount in a sachet, and add it to the flour, never to the liquid. If you add it with the salt, do so on opposite sides of the bowl, as salt (and too much sugar) retards its growth. (And hot water kills it.) If you use too much yeast, the dough will be lively, but the baked loaf may have a strong aftertaste and will go stale more quickly. If you use too little, the dough will take longer to rise and prove, but will have a deeper flavour and most likely keep better.

Conversion Tables

WEIGHT

Metric	Imperial	Metric	Imperial	Metric	Imperial	Metric	Imperial
25g	1oz	200g	7oz	425g	15oz	800g	1lb 12oz
50g	2oz	225g	8oz	450g	1lb	850g	1lb 14oz
75g	2½ oz	250g	9oz	500g	1lb 2oz	900g	2lb
85g	3oz	280g	10oz	550g	1lb 4oz	950g	2lb 2oz
100g	4oz	300g	11oz	600g	1lb 5oz	1kg	2lb 4oz
125g	4½ oz	350g	12oz	650g	1lb 7oz		
140g	5oz	375g	13oz	700g	1lb 9oz		
175g	6oz	400g	14oz	750g	1lb 10oz		

VOLUME

Metric	Imperial	Metric	Imperial	Metric	Imperial	Metric	Imperial
30ml	1fl oz	150ml	¼ pint	300ml	½ pint	500ml	18fl oz
50ml	2fl oz	175ml	6fl oz	350ml	12fl oz	600ml	1 pint
75ml	2½ fl oz	200ml	7fl oz	400ml	14fl oz	700ml	1¼ pints
100ml	3½ fl oz	225ml	8fl oz	425ml	⅔ pint	850ml	1½ pints
125ml	4fl oz	250ml	9fl oz	450ml	16fl oz	1 litre	1¾ pints

LINEAR

Metric	Imperial	Metric	Imperial	Metric	Imperial	Metric	Imperial
5mm	¼in	6cm	2½in	11cm	4¼in	18cm	7in
1cm	½in	7cm	2¾in	12cm	4½in	20cm	8in
2.5cm	1in	7.5cm	3in	13cm	5in	21cm	8¼in
3cm	1¼in	8cm	3¼in	14cm	5½in	22cm	8½in
4cm	1½in	9cm	3½in	15cm	6in	23cm	9in
5cm	2in	9.5cm	3¾in	16cm	6¼in	24cm	9½in
5.5cm	2¼in	10cm	4in	17cm	6½in	25cm	10in

US CUP

Ingredients	1 cup	¾ cup	⅔ cup	½ cup	⅓ cup	¼ cup	2 tbsp
Brown sugar	180g	135g	120g	90g	60g	45g	23g
Butter	240g	180g	160g	120g	80g	60g	30g
Cornflour (cornstarch)	120g	90g	80g	60g	40g	30g	15g
Flour	120g	90g	80g	60g	40g	30g	15g
Icing sugar (powdered/confectioners')	100g	75g	70g	50g	35g	25g	13g
Nuts (chopped)	150g	110g	100g	75g	50g	40g	20g
Nuts (ground)	120g	90g	80g	60g	40g	30g	15g
Oats	90g	65g	60g	45g	30g	22g	11g
Raspberries	120g	90g	80g	60g	40g	30g	--
Salt	300g	230g	200g	150g	100g	75g	40g
Sugar (caster/superfine)	225g	170g	150g	115g	75g	55g	30g
Sugar (granulated)	200g	150g	130g	100g	65g	50g	25g
Sultanas/raisins	200g	150g	130g	100g	65g	50g	22g
Water/milk	250ml	180ml	150ml	120ml	75ml	60ml	30ml

SPOON MEASURES

Metric	Imperial
5ml	1 tsp
10ml	2 tsp
15ml	1 tbsp
30ml	2 tbsp
45ml	3 tbsp
60ml	4 tbsp
75ml	5 tbsp

OVEN TEMPERATURES

°C	°F	Gas	°C	°F	Gas
70	150	¼	180	350	4
100	200	½	190	375	5
110	225	½	200	400	6
130	250	1	210	415	6–7
140	275	1	220	425	7
150	300	2	230	450	8
160	315	2–3	240	475	8
170	325	3	250	500	9

Inspire me…

Use this visual index when you need inspiration for a bake by time of day or occasion. *Wake-up bakes* make delicious breakfasts; *Elevenses* are the bakes to have with a cup of coffee at your desk or over the morning papers; *In (and out) for lunch* features picnic treats, lunchbox staples and bakes for lunchtime gatherings at home; *Afternoon tea* bursts with indulgences fit for teatime with royalty; *Over for dinner* collects gorgeous centrepieces for a dinner party; and *Time for a party* comprises the crowd-pleasers for birthdays, weddings, anniversaries and other celebrations.

Wake-up bakes

Fruit, nut & seed flapjacks (p.71)

Porridge bread (p.74)

Chocolate hazelnut brioche buns (p.76)

French baguettes (p.79)

Cinnamon & raisin milk bread (p.87)

Croissants with praline crème pâtissière (p.133)

Pain Suisse (p.145)

Gluten-free seeded bagels (p.201)

Gluten-free seeded bread (p.209)

Elevenses

Prue's lemon & thyme bundt (p.23)

Blueberry, pecan & cinnamon crumble traybake (p.36)

Ginger crunch ice-cream sandwiches (p.54)

Iced party rings (p.56)

White chocolate, pistachio & cranberry shortbreads (p.59)

Florentine cookies (p.60)

Prue's custard creams (p.62)

Choc-chip cookies (p.64)

Cosmic Neapolitan bites (p.68)

Fruit, nut & seed flapjacks (p.71)

Chocolate hazelnut brioche buns (p.76)

Cheesy leek pastries (p.109)

Elevenses CONTINUED

Croissants with praline crème pâtissière (p.133)

Ginger financiers (p.136)

Double-cherry double-nut tiffin (p.180)

Chocolate & peanut brookies (p.189)

Vegan coffee & walnut cake (p.198)

Dairy & gluten-free lemon cake (p.205)

In (and out) for lunch

Lemon, lime & blackberry
Victoria sponge (p.20)

Blueberry, pecan & cinnamon
crumble traybake (p.36)

Ginger crunch ice-cream
sandwiches (p.54)

Porridge bread (p.74)

French baguettes (p.79)

Kale, pesto & roasted red
pepper babka (p.82)

Feta & za'atar flatbreads
(p.84)

Curry-spiced tear
& share loaf (p.88)

Pear, taleggio & walnut
sourdough focaccia (p.92)

Mini sausage & egg pies
(p.100)

Paul's dauphinoise
potato & caramelised
onion pithivier (p.103)

Med-veg tarte tatin (p.106)

In (and out) for lunch CONTINUED

Cheesy leek pastries (p.109)

Stuffed crust quiche (p.114)

Lamb samosas (p.120)

Apricot curd meringue roulade (p.155)

Summer fruit crumble (p.156)

Rhubarb crumble pots (p.170)

Double-cherry double-nut tiffin (p.180)

Gooey chocolate & caramel tart (p.185)

Chocolate bread & butter pudding (p.190)

Gluten-free seeded bagels (p.201)

Vegan tropical fruit tart (p.206)

Gluten-free seeded bread (p.209)

Afternoon tea

Lemon, lime & blackberry
Victoria sponge (p.20)

Prue's lemon & thyme
bundt (p.23)

Pistachio & raspberry
vertical cake (p.27)

Cherry bakewell fondant
fancies (p.29)

Layered lemon cake (p.33)

Florentine cookies (p.60)

Prue's custard creams
(p.62)

Cinnamon & raisin
milk bread (p.87)

Caramel latte cream puffs
(p.111)

Passion fruit & mango
opera cake (p.127)

Gâteau Concorde (p.129)

Ginger financiers (p.136)

Afternoon tea CONTINUED

Rhubarb & custard mille
feuille (p.141)

Apricot curd meringue
roulade (p.155)

Lemon meringue tarts
(p.167)

Double-trouble chocolate
cake (p.174)

Prue's caramelised white
chocolate & blackcurrant
cheesecakes (p.177)

Black Forest chocolate
mousse cake (p.193)

Vegan blueberry & lemon
cupcakes (p.202)

Gluten-free seeded bread
(p.209)

Gluten-free chocolate
orange macarons (p.214)

Over for dinner

Mini honey bundt cakes
with baked figs (p.42)

Ginger crunch ice-cream
sandwiches (p.54)

Pecorino, walnut & rosemary
shortbreads (p.67)

Curry-spiced tear
& share loaf (p.88)

Dill-pickle brioche
burger buns (p.91)

Pear, taleggio & walnut
sourdough focaccia (p.92)

Curried vegetable pie (p.97)

Med-veg tarte tatin (p.106)

Caramel latte cream puffs
(p.111)

Autumn hedgerow tart
(p.117)

Pear, hazelnut &
chocolate tart (p.122)

Gâteau Concorde (p.129)

Prue's tarte aux pommes
(p.139)

Summer berry charlotte
(p.147)

Paul's ginger & orange
treacle puddings (p.152)

Apricot curd meringue
roulade (p.155)

Over for dinner CONTINUED

St Clement's trifle (p.159)

Salted caramel praline soufflés with hot chocolate sauce (p.163)

Panna cotta tart with berry jelly (p.164)

Lemon meringue tarts (p.167)

Sticky toffee chocolate puddings (p.168)

Rhubarb crumble pots (p.170)

Prue's caramelised white chocolate & blackcurrant cheesecakes (p.177)

Chocolate, hazelnut & almond dacquoise (p.183)

Gooey chocolate & caramel tart (p.185)

Chocolate bread & butter pudding (p.190)

Black Forest chocolate mousse cake (p.193)

Vegan tropical fruit tart (p.206)

Vegan mini pavlovas (p.213)

Time for a party

Lemon, lime & blackberry Victoria sponge (p.20)

Pistachio & raspberry vertical cake (p.27)

Cherry bakewell fondant fancies (p.29)

Layered lemon cake (p.33)

Vanilla, almond & apricot celebration cake (p.39)

Tiered coconut cake (p.45)

Paul's caterpillar cake (p.49)

Ginger crunch ice-cream sandwiches (p.54)

Iced party rings (p.56)

Pecorino, walnut & rosemary shortbreads (p.67)

Cosmic Neapolitan bites (p.68)

Dill-pickle brioche burger buns (p.91)

Time for a party CONTINUED

Mini sausage & egg pies
(p.100)

Lamb samosas (p.120)

Double-trouble chocolate
cake (p.174)

Prue's caramelised white
chocolate & blackcurrant
cheesecakes (p.177)

Vegan coffee & walnut cake
(p.198)

Vegan blueberry & lemon
cupcakes (p.202)

Vegan caramelly chocolate
cupcakes (p.210)

Vegan mini pavlovas
(p.213)

Gluten-free chocolate
orange macarons (p.214)

Index

This book is published to accompany the television series entitled *The Great British Bake Off*, broadcast on Channel 4 in 2023

The Great British Bake Off® is a registered trademark of Love Productions Ltd

Series produced for Channel 4 Television by Love Productions

The Great British Bake Off: Kitchen Classics

First published in Great Britain in 2023 by Sphere

10 9 8 7 6 5 4 3 2 1

Text and recipes © Love Productions Ltd 2023
Design and recipe photography © Little, Brown Book Group 2023
Additional photography © Love Productions Ltd 2023

A CIP catalogue record for this book is available from the British Library.

ISBN: 978-1-4087-2700-3

New recipes developed and written by:
Annie Rigg

Senior Commissioning Editor: Tig Wallace
Design & Art Direction: Smith & Gilmour
Project Editor: Judy Barratt
Copyeditor: Nicola Graimes
Food Photographer: Ant Duncan
On-set Photographer: Smith & Gilmour
Baker Portrait Photographer: Mark Bourdillon
Food Stylist: Annie Rigg
Assistant Food Stylist: Hattie Baker
Props Stylist: Hannah Wilkinson
Hand Models: Hattie Arnold, Ifrah Ismail and Tig Wallace
Production Manager: Abby Marshall
Cover Design: Smith & Gilmour
Vanilla, almond & apricot celebration cake (p.39) developed by Sophie Garwood

Publisher's thanks to: Hilary Bird; Sarah Epton; Tammy and Andy Brown

Typeset in ITC Modern 216 and Sentinel
Colour origination by Born Group
Printed and bound in Italy by L.E.G.O. SpA

Papers used by Sphere are from well-managed forest and other responsible sources.

Sphere
An imprint of Little, Brown Book Group, Carmelite House, 50 Victoria Embankment, London EC4Y 0DZ
An Hachette UK Company
www.hachette.co.uk www.littlebrown.co.uk

WITH THANKS

Love Productions would like to thank the following people:
Executive Producer: Jenna Mansfield
Food & Challenge Producer: Katy Bigley
Home Economist: Becca Watson
Love Executives: Letty Kavanagh, Rupert Frisby, Kieran Smith, Joe Bartley
Publicists: Amanda Console, Shelagh Pymm
Comissioning Editor: Vivienne Molokwu

Thank you also to: Paul, Prue, Noel and Alison. *And to the bakers for their recipes:*
Abbi, Amos, Cristy, Dan, Dana, Josh, Keith, Matty, Nicky, Rowan, Saku and Tasha.